# STRATEGIES FOR HOLIDAY MARKETING SUCCESS

I0446737

Using Christmas Cheer for Business Growth & Tips to Boost Sales in Weeks Given details to take gain & prospects value in millions Dis season using basic sense.

## RICHARD N WILLIAMS

# TABLE OF CONTENTS

# INTRODUCTION

Sofia, a determined entrepreneur, faced the challenge of turning her small business into a holiday cheerleader in the city's bustling center. She embraced the idea of using the Christmas spirit to take her business to new heights as the holiday season approached.

The journey of Sofia began with careful market research. Understanding the beat of her crowd, she distinguished key patterns and shopper inclinations during the Christmas season. She used the information she had gathered to tailor her products to meet the festive needs of her target audience.

Advancement turned into the foundation of Sofia's technique. She worked with local artists to create limited-edition holiday-themed products that had a personal impact on customers. The products were more than just things you could buy; They evolved into tangible manifestations of the season's joy and warmth.

Sofia used the internet to expand her audience. She curated engaging content that not only showcased her festive merchandise but also invited customers into the enchanting world she was creating because she was aware of the power of social media. She made sure that her brand was not only a participant in the holiday conversation but also a trendsetter by using hashtags in a strategic way and advertising to specific audiences.

As orders poured in, Sofia confronted a strategic test. The demand exceeded her expectations and put her small team to their limits. She didn't let that stop her from using technology to make things easier. She made sure that every customer got their holiday treats on time by partnering with a dependable logistics company and putting in place an effective inventory management system.

The foundation of Sofia's success was her team's tenacity. They banded together in the face of difficulties, motivated by the same goal of making their clients happy. Their dedication fostered a positive work environment that permeated all client interactions, spreading goodwill.

Sofia perceived the significance of local area commitment during special times of year. She encouraged partnerships that were to everyone's advantage rather than seeing the businesses that are adjacent to her as rivals. A festive atmosphere was created through joint events, cross-promotions, and marketing initiatives that were shared, drawing customers to the area for the benefit of all parties involved.

Sofia's holiday marketing strategy now relies heavily on the power of storytelling. She conveyed each product's craftsmanship, dedication, and passion through the narrative of her brand. Customers were not merely purchasing goods; They were becoming a part of something greater than a transaction as they invested in a story.

Sofia orchestrated a slew of captivating events throughout the holiday season. She made certain that her brand was not only a seller of products but also a creator of experiences by organizing virtual gatherings that brought the community together and pop-up shops that were decorated with blinking lights. A sense of connection that transcended the transactional nature of business was created through these events, which acted as touchpoints.

Sofia was able to use customer feedback as a compass to steer her way. She effectively looked for audits, tributes, and ideas, utilizing them to refine her contributions and further develop client experience. She demonstrated that her brand was a dynamic entity that was constantly evolving to meet the needs of its patrons by listening to her audience. In addition to building a loyal customer base, she did this by listening to them.

In the end, Sofia's successful holiday marketing strategies did more than just increase sales; They demonstrated the transformative potential of creativity, perseverance, and community spirit. Her once-sparse enterprise had grown into a beacon of holiday cheer, not only contributing to the festive atmosphere but also making an indelible impression on customers' hearts.

As the Christmas season attracted her, Sofia considered her excursion.

Which began as a dream had bloomed into an account of win over difficulties, a story of an independent venture exploring the cutthroat scene and arising more grounded. Her future endeavors will be guided by the lessons she gained, including the significance of innovation, the strength of resilience, and the impact of genuine community engagement.

Sofia's story stood out as a shining example of what could be accomplished when passion, creativity, and a dash of Christmas cheer combined harmoniously in the tapestry of holiday marketing success.

# Overview of Holiday Marketing

Businesses' overall marketing strategies include holiday marketing, which is a dynamic and essential component. Companies have a one-of-a-kind chance to engage with their target audience and increase sales during this time of year, which is frequently marked by increased consumer spending and festive sentiments. The outline of occasion promoting envelopes different perspectives, including the meaning of the Christmas season for organizations, key techniques utilized, and the developing scene in the advanced time.

**The Importance of the Holidays:**

For businesses in all sectors, the holiday season is very important. Generally starting around Thanksgiving and reaching out through New Year's Day, this period observes a flood in purchaser spending. People are much of the time feeling happy, effectively looking for items and administrations for individual use or as gifts. This presents an excellent opportunity for businesses to increase revenue, increase customer loyalty, and increase brand visibility.

**Important Holiday Marketing Techniques:**

**Campaigns with a Theme:**

By designing thematic campaigns that are relevant to the holiday season, brands capitalize on the festive mood. Aligning marketing efforts with the celebration's theme creates an emotional connection with customers, whether it's Christmas, Hanukkah, Diwali, or another occasion. This may entail incorporating holiday traditions, colors, and symbols into marketing and advertising materials.

**Special Discounts and Offers:**

The need to keep moving related with the Christmas season prompts purchasers to look for exceptional arrangements and limits. Package deals, limited-time offers, and exclusive promotions all draw attention and boost sales. Countdowns and promotional calendars are frequently used to build anticipation and encourage customers to make purchases at the right time.

**Multichannel advertising:**

With the multiplication of computerized stages, organizations carry out multichannel promoting procedures to contact a more extensive crowd. This incorporates internet publicizing, online entertainment crusades, email advertising, and conventional techniques like print and TV advertisements. A firm methodology guarantees reliable informing across different channels, expanding the effect on buyers.

**Personalization:**

Customized showcasing encounters resound well with shoppers. Engaging content, offers, and recommendations that are tailored to individual preferences during the holiday season. This can be accomplished with insights based on data, such as information about a person's demographics, shopping habits, and past purchases.

**Engagement on Social Media:**

Web-based entertainment stages become especially powerful during special times of year. Through contests, interactive campaigns, and creative and shareable content, brands actively engage with their audience. The reach and authenticity of marketing efforts can be enhanced by user-generated content that features holiday experiences with the brand.

**Optimisation for Mobile:**

Optimizing marketing strategies for mobile platforms is essential as mobile usage continues to rise. A seamless shopping experience is made possible by responsive design, mobile apps, and mobile-friendly websites. Promotions and advertisements geared toward mobile devices target customers who increasingly value the ease of smartphone shopping.

**Change in the Digital Age:**

The landscape of holiday marketing has been reshaped by digital technology. During this time of year, e-commerce platforms, social media, and data analytics play crucial roles in shaping and enhancing marketing strategies.

**Dominance of e-commerce:**

Holiday marketing has been significantly affected by the rise of online shopping. During the holidays, e-commerce platforms see an increase in traffic and transactions, making it crucial for businesses to have a strong online presence. Offering free internet shopping encounters, secure exchanges, and solid conveyance administrations add to consumer loyalty.

**Personalization and Analytics of Data:**

The accessibility of immense measures of shopper information permits organizations to adjust their vacation showcasing techniques. Information examination assist with distinguishing patterns, inclinations, and buyer ways of behaving, empowering customized promoting approaches. Designated ads and suggestions in light of prescient examination add to additional viable and proficient missions.

**Marketing with Influencers:**

During the holidays, influencer marketing has become more popular. Reach and credibility can be increased by collaborating with influencers who share a brand's values and target audience. Influencers influence the purchasing decisions of their followers by sharing product recommendations, reviews, and engaging content.

Virtual Reality (VR) and augmented reality (AR):

Holiday marketing campaigns are increasingly incorporating cutting-edge technologies like augmented reality and virtual reality. Customer engagement is increased by immersive shopping experiences, interactive product displays, and virtual try-ons. The brand stands out in a crowded market thanks to the excitement and differentiation provided by these technologies.

The overview of holiday marketing highlights its strategic significance for businesses hoping to take advantage of the holiday season. Companies can create memorable experiences for customers, foster brand loyalty, and achieve substantial revenue growth during this crucial period by aligning with the spirit of the holidays, employing key marketing strategies, and adapting to the dynamics of the digital era.

# Importance of Leveraging Christmas Cheer

Utilizing holiday spirit isn't just about praising an occasion; It's about making the most of the festive spirit and positive energy that this time of year brings. There are numerous reasons why individuals, communities, and businesses should actively participate in and promote the significance of leveraging Christmas cheer, in addition to the joy and festivities.

Christmas cheer first and foremost cultivates a sense of belonging and community. The holiday season has a special capacity for bringing people closer together, encouraging them to put aside their differences and unite in a spirit of love and goodwill. Whether it's through family social affairs, local area occasions, or working environment festivities, the common delight of Christmas makes bonds and associations that can persevere past the Christmas season.

Christmas cheer can have a significant impact on employee morale and team dynamics in the context of businesses. The holiday season offers a chance to lighten the mood in a workplace that can frequently be stressful and demanding. Coordinating merry exercises, beautifications, and group building occasions during this time can establish a positive and strong workplace. Employees who are appreciated and connected are more likely to be engaged and productive, which contributes to a workplace culture that is healthier and more vibrant.

Additionally, holiday cheer enhances overall well-being. People typically place a greater emphasis on acts of kindness, giving, and gratitude during the holiday season. Participating in beneficent exercises, chipping in, or basically spreading thoughtfulness and liberality can emphatically affect mental and profound prosperity. Studies have offered that demonstrations of grace discharge endorphins, advancing a feeling of joy and satisfaction.

From a psychological point of view, using Christmas cheer to fight the winter blues or seasonal affective disorder (SAD) that some people get during the colder months can also be helpful. The merry lights, improvements, and the overall air of euphoria related with Christmas can go about as mind-set promoters, reducing side effects of occasional wretchedness.

Moreover, the monetary effect of holiday spirit ought to be considered carefully. Businesses, particularly those in the retail sector, rely heavily on the holiday season. Businesses can take advantage of the fact that consumers are typically in a mood to give and spend more by offering special promotions, discounts, and festive products. In addition to assisting individual businesses, this uptick in economic activity also benefits the economy as a whole.

During the Christmas season, in addition to individual businesses, the tourism industry also experiences an uptick. In order to spend the holidays or spend time with their families, many people travel. This influx of tourists brings in money for the local economies, which helps businesses and creates jobs.

On a larger scale, spreading holiday cheer can contribute to the development of a positive and harmonious society. The qualities related with Christmas, like sympathy, compassion, and liberality, can add to a more empathetic and interconnected local area. Small or large acts of kindness spread throughout society, fostering a culture of compassion and understanding.

Additionally, the holiday season facilitates cultural understanding and exchange. Individuals from different foundations and convictions meet up to celebrate, establishing a climate where variety is embraced and contrasts are saved. In the long run, cultural inclusivity may result in a more harmonious coexistence and foster tolerance.

The significance of spreading holiday cheer far outweighs the superficial celebrations. It discusses the development of communities, employee well-being, economic expansion, and social harmony. Taking advantage of the festive atmosphere can have a lasting impact, spreading feelings of joy, kindness, and community. Christmas cheer can contribute to a world that is more alive, connected, and compassionate, whether on an individual, corporate, or societal level.

# Chapter 1 Understanding Your Audience

Understanding your crowd is a pivotal part of successful correspondence. Whether you're creating a convincing exposition, conveying a discourse, or making content for a site, fitting your message to reverberate with your crowd can have the effect among progress and haziness.

The first step in any communication plan is to determine your target audience. Take into account factors like age, gender, education, and occupation. These variables shape individuals' points of view and inclinations. For example, a show focused on youthful experts could embrace a more casual tone and utilize contemporary references, while a talk for scholastics could dive into inside and out research and complex wording.

Additionally, it is essential to comprehend your audience's psychographics. Examining attitudes, values, interests, and lifestyles are all part of this. Are they liberal or conservative? Traditional or technology-savvy? You can create a connection that goes beyond surface-level demographics by aligning your message with their beliefs and preferences by identifying these aspects.

Another crucial aspect is cultural awareness. Sensitivities, humor, and communication styles are influenced by cultural nuances. In some cultures, what is acceptable may be offensive in others. Your message will have a greater impact and relevance if you acknowledge and respect these differences. This is especially significant in our interconnected world, where messages can contact assorted worldwide crowds.

Besides, understanding your crowd's information level is fundamental. Tailor your substance to match their ability. When addressing experts, be careful not to oversimplify, but avoid jargon and overly technical language when addressing the general public. Finding the right balance makes sure that your message is easy to understand and interesting.

Compassion assumes a critical part in understanding your crowd. Consider their concerns, put yourself in their shoes, and anticipate their inquiries. This not only improves your comprehension but also helps you connect with others. Trust and receptivity to your message are cultivated when you demonstrate that you comprehend and value the perspective of your audience.

It's also important how your audience processes the information. A message that reverberates in one setting could crash and burn in another. Take into account the constraints on time, the physical environment, and competing distractions. Tailor your methodology in like manner, whether it's catching consideration in an uproarious public space or conveying a definite report during an engaged gathering.

Moreover, perceiving the close to home condition of your crowd is central. The way information is received and processed can be influenced by emotions. Are they enthusiastic, nervous, or apathetic? Create an atmosphere that is more receptive to your message by adjusting your tone and content to match their emotional state.

Surveys and interactions on social media are two examples of feedback mechanisms that can help you learn more about your audience's preferences and opinions. Effectively look for and break down input to refine your correspondence procedure. This iterative cycle guarantees that your message keeps on reverberating with your developing crowd.

Capturing and keeping attention is a valuable commodity in the digital age, where information overload is a constant challenge. Understanding your crowd's media utilization propensities is vital. Is it true or not that they are ardent perusers, visual students, or sound aficionados? Tailor your substance arrangement to line up with their inclinations. This might entail making engaging videos, incorporating compelling images, or producing informative podcasts.

Additionally, a crucial consideration is your audience's rate of information processing. Some individuals may value a thorough examination of specifics while others value a concise summary. You can accommodate a diverse audience by offering both options, allowing everyone to engage with your message in a manner that best suits their preferences.

Your audience changes with societal values and trends. To remain relevant, regularly evaluate and update your understanding of your audience. Maintain the effectiveness of your communication strategies in the face of shifting dynamics by adopting a mindset that is open to continuous learning and adaptation.

it is necessary to examine demographics, psychographics, culture, knowledge level, empathy, context, emotions, feedback, media habits, and the changing nature of your audience in order to fully comprehend them. You will not only increase the impact of your communication but also create connections with those you want to engage that will last a lifetime if you put in the time and effort to develop this understanding.

# Identifying Target Demographics

A crucial component of any successful marketing strategy is determining the demographics of the target audience. Understanding the preferences, characteristics, and behaviors of the audience you want to reach is necessary. Businesses can tailor their messages and offerings to better resonate with specific demographics, thereby increasing their chances of market success.

Conducting thorough market research is an essential step in determining the demographics of your target audience. This requires gathering information on a variety of factors, including age, gender, income level, location, and lifestyle choices. Businesses can visualize and comprehend their ideal customers by analyzing this data, which contributes to the creation of comprehensive customer profiles.

Understanding the age gathering of your ideal interest group is fundamental. Preferences, interests, and purchasing patterns vary by age group. For instance, while baby boomers may place a higher value on dependability and familiarity, millennials might be more interested in sustainability and technology. Businesses can tailor their products, messaging, and advertising channels based on these generational differences.

Another important demographic factor is gender. Because of societal expectations, preferences, and cultural influences, products and services frequently appeal to men and women in different ways. Making marketing messages that resonate with the specific gender demographics you want to target is easier when you are aware of these subtleties.

A key factor in determining purchasing power is income level. Pricing strategies and product positioning are made easier by determining your target audience's income range. Major league salary people might be more intrigued by premium or extravagant items, while those with lower livelihoods could focus on reasonableness and worth.

Consumer behavior is significantly influenced by geographical location. Social, financial, and environment contrasts can impact what items and administrations are popular in unambiguous locales. Relevance and appeal can be enhanced by adapting marketing strategies to the local context. Hobbies, interests, and values are all included in lifestyle choices. Recognizing the way of life inclinations of your interest group permits you to adjust your image to their qualities, making a more profound association. For instance, if your target audience is concerned about the environment, putting an emphasis in your marketing on products and procedures that are friendly to the environment can be very effective.

Personality traits, beliefs, and actions are examined by psychographic factors. Understanding your target audience's psychographics reveals their motivations and decision-making processes. Using this information, you can come up with compelling marketing messages that will pique the emotions of your customers.

Businesses can effectively reach their audience through a variety of channels once the demographics of their target audience have been determined. For instance, demographic, interest, and behavior-based targeting options are available on social media platforms. This permits organizations to fit their commercials to explicit crowd fragments.

Another powerful method for reaching the demographics you want to reach is email marketing. Businesses can send personalized messages that are more likely to resonate with recipients by segmenting email lists based on demographic data. Engagement is more likely to occur when there is a sense of connection and relevance created by personalization.

The reach of marketing campaigns can be increased by working with influencers who are similar to the people who have been identified as the target demographic. Influencers provide a direct route to potential customers because they frequently have a dedicated following that closely matches the characteristics of the intended audience.

For ongoing refinement, it is essential to analyze data and measure marketing campaigns' efficacy. Key execution pointers (KPIs, for example, transformation rates, navigate rates, and client securing costs give important bits of knowledge into the progress of focusing on techniques. Marketing efforts remain in line with the changing requirements and preferences of the target demographics if they are regularly reevaluated and modified in light of these metrics.

developing a successful marketing strategy begins with determining the demographics of the target audience.

Businesses can gain valuable insights into the characteristics, preferences, and behaviors of their ideal customers by conducting comprehensive market research. With this knowledge, products, messages, and marketing strategies can be tailored to effectively reach and appeal to the intended audience, resulting in market success.

# Analyzing Consumer Behavior During the Holidays

The fascinating topic of holiday consumer behavior examines the intricate ways in which individuals and households navigate the festive season's commercial landscape. The Christmas season, frequently set apart by Thanksgiving, Christmas, Hanukkah, and New Year's festivals, changes shopper propensities and inclinations, affecting all that from buying choices to mark unwaveringly. Businesses looking to take advantage of the holiday spirit need to have a solid understanding of the dynamics of consumer behavior during this time period.

The emotional connection to holidays is one of the main factors that influence consumer behavior. Joy, nostalgia, stress, and anxiety are just a few of the feelings that the holidays can elicit. Purchasers frequently look for items and encounters that line up with these profound triggers. Branding that evokes fond memories or products that claim to ease holiday stress, for instance, can have a powerful impact on customers.

Giving gifts is a big part of what people do during the holidays. As individuals search for the ideal presents for friends and family, they engage in an increased level of shopping. This pursuit frequently increases an individual's willingness to investigate new premium brands. By appealing to customers' desire for one-of-a-kind and meaningful gifts with holiday-specific editions, bundle deals, and exclusive promotions, retailers strategically exploit this tendency.

Besides, the Christmas season is set apart by a flood of get-togethers and merriments. This social aspect has a significant impact on consumer behavior, driving food, decoration, and entertainment-related purchases. Home decor, party supplies, and specialty foods are all popular investments among consumers during the holiday season. Brands that adjust their items to the social parts of special times of year can effectively catch the consideration of customers hoping to improve their celebratory encounters.

It is impossible to overstate the impact of digital platforms on holiday consumer behavior. The way people shop for the holidays has changed as a result of the rise of e-commerce. Online shopping makes things easier, gives you access to more products, and makes it easy to compare prices. Increasing their online presence, providing exclusive online deals, and optimizing user experiences on their websites and mobile apps are some of the ways retailers adapt. The incorporation of social media also plays a significant role because consumers further influence their decisions regarding holiday shopping by drawing inspiration from peers and influencers.

During the holidays, price sensitivity shifts. While buyers might be more cost cognizant during standard seasons, special times of year frequently see a readiness to spend all the more openly. It becomes common to think of "treating oneself" or buying expensive goods for special occasions. Businesses can capitalize on the consumer's altered perception of value during the holiday season by introducing luxury goods or premium services as a result of this shift in price sensitivity.

When it comes to holiday marketing, scarcity and urgency strategies become potent tools. The holiday season's inherent sense of urgency is tapped into by countdown deals, limited-time promotions, and exclusive holiday releases. Impulsive purchases are more common among customers who are motivated by the fear of missing out on exclusive deals or products. During this time of increased consumer activity, businesses strategically create a sense of scarcity to increase demand and sales.

Consumer behavior during the holiday season is also influenced by the idea of experiential gifts. Customers are increasingly valuing experiences as gifts rather than only material possessions. Experiential offerings like spa days, concert tickets, and travel packages have grown in popularity as a result of this shift. Recognizing that consumers are looking for ways to create memories that will last a lifetime during the holiday season, companies that offer opportunities for unique and memorable experiences capitalize on this trend.

A complex interplay of emotions, social dynamics, and shifting preferences is revealed when analyzing holiday consumer behavior. Businesses can tailor their marketing strategies to appeal to customers during this holiday season if they comprehend and adapt to these dynamics. Successful holiday marketing necessitates a nuanced comprehension of the factors that shape consumer behavior during this joyous time of year. This includes using emotional connections to emphasize gift-giving customs, embracing digital platforms, and creating promotions driven by scarcity.

# Chapter 2
# Crafting Festive Campaigns

The art of creating festive campaigns transcends traditional marketing boundaries. It requires a delicate balance of creativity, strategic thinking, and comprehension of the holiday sentiments of the target audience. Whether it's Christmas, Hanukkah, Diwali, or some other festival, organizations can exploit the bubbly soul to draw in with clients and upgrade brand mindfulness. Here is a nitty gritty investigation of the key perspectives engaged with creating fruitful merry missions.

**Figuring out the Crowd:**

Prior to jumping into the inventive approach, understanding the crowd's social and profound setting during the merry season is essential. It is essential to tailor campaigns to resonate with the sentiments of various communities, as distinct celebrations have distinct meanings for different communities. Aligning the campaign with the festival's values creates a more genuine connection, whether it's focusing on family, traditions, or gift-giving.

**A festive approach to storytelling:**

Happy missions give a remarkable chance to recount convincing stories that bring out feelings and resound with the crowd. Consolidating stories that line up with the soul of the time can have an enduring effect. For instance, a mission based on the delight of giving or inspiring family minutes can make a feeling of association and generosity.

**Branding and aesthetics of the visual:**

A festive campaign's visual appeal is crucial to attracting attention. Including holiday-themed colors, images, and symbols in branding helps to create a cohesive and immersive experience.

Consistency across different touchpoints, including online entertainment, email, and actual stores, builds up the brand's happy character.

**Creative Advancements and Limits:**

Businesses can take advantage of the fact that shopping is synonymous with the holiday season by providing innovative discounts and promotions. Restricted time offers, selective merry packs, or imaginative limits attached to occasion subjects can boost clients to make buys.

Promos in the form of a countdown or advent calendar create a sense of anticipation and encourage repeat visits to see what comes next.

**Intuitive Missions and Client Commitment:**

Drawing in clients through intelligent missions catches their eye as well as supports cooperation. User-generated content contests, quizzes, and contests with festive themes can raise brand awareness and create buzz. Empowering clients to share their vacation stories or encounters connected with the brand can encourage a feeling of locality.

**Promotion on Social Media:**

Online entertainment stages are amazing assets for enhancing merry missions. The campaign's reach can be increased by making use of festival-related hashtags, sharing content, and user-generated content. The impact is maximized by tailoring content to each platform's strengths, whether it's engaging polls on Twitter or visually appealing images on Instagram.

**Offers and Personalized Messaging:**

Personalization adds a touch of exclusivity to festive campaigns and makes customers feel valued. Fitting information in view of past buy history or giving customized offers adds a layer of complexity to the mission. Tending to clients by name and sending customized good tidings improves the general client experience.

## Multi-Channel Showcasing:

An effective merry mission ought to traverse across different showcasing channels. Maximizing visibility is made possible by combining offline and online strategies. From computerized promoting and email showcasing to in-store shows and customary media, a strong methodology across various channels builds up the bubbly message and improves the probability of contacting a different crowd.

## Rewarding the Local area:

Businesses can also take advantage of festive campaigns to give back to the community. The brand is aligned with a sense of social responsibility by incorporating charitable initiatives or partnering with local organizations for festive-themed charity events. In addition to fostering goodwill, this establishes a positive connection between the community and the brand.

## Estimating and Dissecting Effort Achievement:

To guarantee the viability of a bubbly mission, it's essential to lay out key execution markers (KPIs) and track the mission's prosperity. Measurements, for example, expanded site traffic, commitment via web-based entertainment, change rates, and deals can give significant experiences.

Businesses can learn what worked well and where they can improve their campaigns in the future by analyzing the data.

All in all, making bubbly missions includes a fastidious mix of imagination, social responsiveness, and vital preparation. Businesses can create memorable and impactful festive campaigns by comprehending the audience, embracing visual aesthetics, offering novel promotions, engaging users across channels, and giving back to the community.

The emotional connection that customers form with each other during these special occasions of celebration is what makes a business successful, not just the products or services it provides.

# Designing Holiday-Themed Content

Planning occasion themed content is an innovative undertaking that permits organizations and people to interface with their crowd on an additional individual and bubbly level. Whether it's for web-based entertainment, sites, email crusades, or actual materials, mixing your substance with occasional soul can catch consideration and make a paramount encounter. We'll look at important things to think about, popular design elements, and effective ways to make your holiday visuals stand out in this look at designing content with a holiday theme.

**Getting to Know Your Audience:**
Understanding your target audience is the first step in creating holiday-themed

content. Various occasions appeal to various socioeconomics, and realizing who you're focusing on helps tailor your plans likewise. Age, cultural background, and location are all important considerations. For instance, despite the fact that Christmas is a holiday that is celebrated all over the world, the manner in which it is observed varies greatly between cultures. This knowledge ensures that your content reaches the intended audience.

**Branding that stays the same with a holiday twist:**

Keeping up with brand consistency is vital, in any event, while consolidating occasion subjects. Your holiday content ought to be consistent with the colors, fonts, and overall design of your brand. Adding an occasion turn could mean consolidating occasional varieties, happy symbolism, or topical components that supplement your image character. This consistency enables you to participate in the holiday spirit while also enhancing your brand.

**Palette of Seasonal Colors:**

In design with a holiday theme, colors play a big role. The color scheme associated with each holiday is distinct. For instance, Christmas is frequently connected with red, green, and white, while Halloween inclines towards orange, dark, and purple. Utilizing these customary varieties helps immediately convey the occasion and evokes a happy environment. However, if you want to keep your unique touch, don't be afraid to try new variations or creative ways to incorporate your brand colors.

### Icons and images that captivate:

Visuals are at the core of occasion themed content. Make use of captivating images that capture the essence of the holiday. This might include Christmas-themed ornaments, presents, or trees that have been decorated. Pumpkins, witches, or other spooky elements may be included in Halloween designs. Coordinate occasion themed symbols to improve the visual allure, making your substance more unmistakable and shareable.

### Christmas-themed typography:

Typography is one more useful asset for conveying the occasional soul. Consider consolidating happy text styles or adding embellishing components to your standard typography. Play around with styles that make you feel the way the holiday makes you feel, like the elegant look of script fonts for Christmas or the spooky fun of bold lettering for Halloween. Finding some kind of harmony among comprehensibility and topical style guarantees your message is successfully imparted.

### Making Shareable Substance:

The holidays are a time for connection and sharing. Plan your substance in light of shareability. Foster visuals that reverberate with feelings, whether it's happiness, wistfulness, or fervor. By launching contests or challenges with holiday themes, you can encourage user-generated content. As people share their holiday creations with their social networks, this not only increases engagement but also broadens the reach of your content.

### Adapting to Different Platforms:

Your holiday content ought to be adaptable because different platforms have different design requirements. Make sure your designs are optimized for every channel you use, including social media, websites, email newsletters, and others. This may necessitate developing distinct versions of your content to meet the needs of each platform. Your brand will be strengthened and your audience will have a cohesive holiday experience if your theme and message are consistent across platforms.

**The key is when:**

The planning of your vacation themed content is pivotal. Plan your plans well ahead of time to line up with the Christmas season. This not only enables you to produce content of a high quality, but it also ensures that it reaches your audience when they are actively looking for information or products related to the holiday season. Be aware of social contrasts and changing occasion plans, particularly assuming your crowd is worldwide.

**Estimating and Examining Execution:**

Subsequent to executing your vacation themed content, break down its exhibition. Use investigation devices to gauge commitment, navigate rates, and social offers. Assess the effectiveness of various design elements and adjust your strategy for subsequent vacations. Gaining from the exhibition of your vacation content improves your capacity to make more compelling and effective plans from here on out.

creating holiday-themed content requires a combination of imagination, planning, and comprehension of your target audience. You can create compelling content that captures the festive spirit and resonates with your audience by maintaining brand consistency, utilizing seasonal colors, engaging imagery, thematic typography, and optimizing for various platforms. Keep in mind, the key is to make a paramount and charming experience for your crowd during the Christmas season.

# Creating Compelling Seasonal Offers

Businesses make a strategic effort to create compelling seasonal offers in order to captivate their audience, increase sales, and cultivate customer loyalty. A well-designed seasonal offer can distinguish a brand from rivals and leave a lasting impression, regardless of the occasion—the holiday season, the back-to-school period, or any other. Let's take a closer look at the important steps in making such offers and how they affect how well a marketing strategy does overall.

Understanding Your Target Market A thorough understanding of your target market is the cornerstone of any seasonal promotion that is successful. Knowing their inclinations, ways of behaving, and buying designs empowers you to tailor your proposals to resound with their requirements. Analyzing customer data, conducting market research, and staying up to date on industry trends all provide valuable insights into what will appeal to your audience in particular seasons.

The effectiveness of a seasonal offer frequently rests on its timing. Timing is everything. Your audience is more likely to engage with your brand if your promotions coincide with relevant holidays, events, or trends. For instance, taking advantage of consumer needs and expectations is to launch a back-to-school sale or offer discounts on winter clothing as the cooler months approach.

**Personalization and Eliteness**

Fitting proposals to individual inclinations adds a customized touch that reverberates with clients. Use information investigation to section your crowd and make designated advancements in view of their buy history, area, or other pertinent elements. Moreover, presenting select arrangements or restricted time offers makes a need to get moving, spurring clients to act quickly to exploit the unique deal.

Effective communication of the value of your seasonal offer necessitates the creation of a compelling message. Underline the advantages clients will acquire, whether it's investment funds, novel items, or a restricted time insight. Consistency in informing across different showcasing channels, including virtual entertainment, email crusades, and in-store shows, supports the proposition and reinforces brand review.

**Cross-Selling and Bundle Deals** Increasing the appeal of seasonal offers can be accomplished through cross-selling and bundle deals. Joining related items or administrations at a limited rate urges clients to investigate a more extensive scope of contributions. This builds the typical exchange esteem as well as acquaints clients with reciprocal things they might not have thought about in any case.

**Presentation and Engaging Visuals** Humans are naturally visual creatures, and captivating visuals are a crucial part of making seasonal offers appealing. Put resources into excellent pictures, designs, and recordings that feature your items or administrations with regards to the season. To attract attention and elicit the desired emotional response, create a presentation that is both cohesive and pleasing to the eye across all marketing channels.

**Collaborations between Influencers and Social** Media In the current digital landscape, it is essential to utilize the power of social media. Foster a virtual entertainment system that expands your compass during occasional advancements. Draw in with your crowd through intuitive substance, challenges, and client created content. Working together with powerhouses who line up with your image adds believability and can fundamentally enhance your message.

**Estimating and Adjusting**
The progress of occasional offers is not entirely settled by their execution yet additionally by the capacity to gauge their effect and adjust appropriately. To evaluate your offers' efficacy, use key

performance indicators (KPIs) like sales data, website traffic, and customer feedback. Improve your strategy for subsequent seasonal campaigns by taking lessons from both successes and failures.

**Building Long-Term Relationships** While the immediate impact of seasonal offers is often to increase short-term sales, the long-term impact is in building relationships with customers over time. Make the most of these chances to make your customers happy and earn their loyalty for years to come. Dependability programs, customized subsequent meet-ups, and present buy commitment contribute to a client driven approach that delivers profits after some time.

Understanding your audience, timing, personalization, creative messaging, visual appeal, and utilizing digital channels are all important aspects of creating compelling seasonal offers. Via cautiously coordinating these components, organizations might not just drive at any point transient deals yet in addition develop persevering through associations with their client base. Occasional offers, when executed nicely, become conditional occasions as well as necessary parts of a brand's story and client commitment system.

# Chapter 3
# Utilizing
# Social Media

The way individuals and businesses connect, communicate, and engage with one another has been transformed as a result of the widespread use of social media, which has transformed how people and businesses interact with one another. This powerful tool is now more than just a place to talk to people; it's a multifaceted tool that has big effects on many different aspects of society.

Virtual entertainment fills in as a unique extension that associates individuals universally, encouraging correspondence and separating geological boundaries. People can share their encounters, contemplations, and thoughts immediately, making a virtual space where different viewpoints merge. This interconnectedness has led to a globalized computerized local area, where social trade and cross-line joint effort flourish.

Social media provides a means of self-expression and identity formation from a personal perspective. Stages like Instagram, Twitter, and TikTok empower clients to organize their computerized personas, sharing parts of their lives through photographs, recordings, and announcements. This self-show has suggestions for individual marking and online standing, impacting how people are seen by their companions and the more extensive web-based local area.

In the expert domain, virtual entertainment has turned into a basic device for systems administration and professional success. Professionals can showcase their skills, connect with others who share their interests, and investigate job opportunities on platforms like LinkedIn. Managers utilize virtual entertainment to vet possible competitors, making areas of strength for a presence an important resource in the present cutthroat work market.

Social media is used strategically by large and small businesses alike for marketing and brand promotion. Traditional marketing strategies have been transformed by the capability of targeting content to a large audience. Online entertainment promoting permits organizations to fit their messages to explicit socioeconomics, augmenting the effect of their missions. Real-time interaction with customers through comments, likes, and shares also fosters customer loyalty by fostering a sense of community around a brand.

In addition, campaigns to raise awareness and spread information rely heavily on social media. Platforms like Twitter can be used as quick channels of communication in times of crisis or emergency, providing real-time updates and connecting people in need with help. Besides, web-based entertainment has been instrumental in bringing issues to light about friendly issues, empowering grassroots developments to pick up speed and prepare support on a worldwide scale.

The use of social media raises concerns regarding privacy, mental health, and the dissemination of false information, despite its numerous benefits. The consistent availability worked with by these stages can add to sensations of separation and nervousness, and the organized idea of online substance might prompt ridiculous correlations and confidence issues. In addition, the speed with which information is shared on social media can lead to the spread of false information and misinformation, which can compromise the accuracy of information.

To outfit the positive parts of virtual entertainment while moderating its disadvantages, people and associations should take on a careful and mindful methodology. Understanding and using privacy settings, promoting digital wellness, and critically evaluating the information shared and consumed online are all part of this. Users will need to be taught media literacy in order to be able to tell the difference between reliable and questionable sources.

An effective social media strategy for businesses requires striking a careful balance between genuine engagement and promotion. Building a veritable internet based presence requires predictable correspondence, responsiveness, and a promise to straightforwardness. Organizations that effectively pay attention to client input and adjust to changing patterns encourage a feeling of trust and unwavering ness among their crowd.

New opportunities and challenges continue to emerge in the social media landscape's ever-evolving landscape.

Innovative methods for connecting and communicating between individuals and businesses are emerging as a result of technological advancements in new platforms and features. New opportunities for immersive and interactive experiences arise from the incorporation of cutting-edge technologies like augmented reality, virtual reality, and others into social media platforms.

from personal relationships to professional endeavors, the use of social media has permeated every aspect of contemporary life. Its effect is certain, forming the manner in which we convey, share data, and assemble associations. Even though social media offers a lot of opportunities, it's important to use it responsibly, with a commitment to making online experiences better, and with ethical considerations. As society keeps on exploring the computerized scene, the dependable use of virtual entertainment will assume an urgent part in forming an associated, informed, and enabled worldwide local area.

# Strategies for Engaging Holiday Audiences

Creativity, empathy, and strategic planning need to be thoughtfully combined in order to engage holiday audiences. Whether you're a business expecting to help deals during the bubbly season or a substance maker trying to interface with your crowd, executing powerful techniques can have a tremendous effect. Here are a few critical ways to deal with consider:

**1. Themed Content Creation:**
Creating occasion themed content resounds well with crowds during this merry time. Tailor your informing, visuals, and tone to line up with the occasion soul. This could entail creating seasonal-themed blog posts, videos, or content for social media that reflects the season's feelings.

**2. Special Holiday Deals:**
By offering exclusive promotions, discounts, or bundle deals during the holidays, you can take advantage of the mindset of consumers. Customers are more likely to take advantage of the special holiday deals when limited-time offers make them feel like they must act quickly. Guarantee that these advancements line up with your image picture and values to keep up with realness.

**3. Interactive Advertising:**
Cultivate commitment through intuitive missions that welcome support from your crowd. Challenges, surveys, and tests connected with occasion topics can engage as well as support client produced content. Participation by users fosters a sense of community and strengthens the connection between the audience and the brand.

**4. Marketing that is customized:**
Make use of data to tailor your marketing efforts. Adapt your messages to the preferences, previous purchases, or actions of your customers. Personalization improves the client experience and makes your image

stand apart in the midst of the torrent of occasion advancements.

## 5. Include Content Contributed by Users:

Your audience should be encouraged to share their holiday memories using your product or service. As genuine testimonials, user-generated content aids in establishing trust. To encourage users to share stories, photos, or videos that are related to your brand, create specialized hashtags and prompts.

## 6. Online Entertainment Commitment:

Engage your audience actively to boost your social media presence. Run polls with holiday themes, respond promptly to comments, and provide behind-the-scenes glimpses of your holiday preparations. A dynamic platform for interaction and feedback in real time is provided by social media.

## 7. User-Friendly on Mobile:

With a rising number of clients getting content through cell phones, enhance your internet based presence for portable. Guarantee that your site, messages, and promoting materials are dynamic to give a consistent encounter to clients in a hurry.

## 8. Force to be reckoned with Joint efforts:

Establish a partnership with influencers who share your brand's values. Your holiday messages can be effectively amplified by influencers, adding a touch of authenticity and relatability to your campaigns. Sponsored posts and collaborative content creation are two examples of influencer collaborations.

## 9. Profound Narrating:

Create stories that touch people's hearts and bring out the holiday spirit. Share stories that inspire happiness, sentimentality, or a feeling of harmony. Individuals are bound to draw in with content that evokes compelling feelings, making narrating an amazing asset during the happy season.

**10. Omnichannel Experience in One:**
Guarantee a reliable brand insight across all channels, whether it's your site, virtual entertainment, or actual stores. During the holidays, a seamless omnichannel strategy reinforces your brand's message by providing your audience with a unified experience.

engaging holiday audiences necessitates a multifaceted strategy that incorporates imagination, individualization, and a thorough comprehension of your target audience. By carrying out these techniques, you might not just catch consideration during the bubbly season at any point yet in addition fabricate enduring associations that reach out past special times of year.

# Leveraging Hashtags and Trends

In the ever-changing social media landscape, using hashtags and trends is a powerful strategy. Since their introduction on Twitter, hashtags have spread to include Instagram, Facebook, and LinkedIn as well. Users are able to find and engage with content that is relevant to their interests thanks to these digital signposts. Your online presence and engagement can be significantly enhanced if you know how to use hashtags effectively and ride the current trends.

Right off the bat, hashtags classify content, making it discoverable to a more extensive crowd. At the point when clients search or snap on a hashtag, they are given a feed of posts utilizing that particular tag. Decisively consolidating applicable and famous hashtags in your posts improves the probability of arriving at clients keen on comparative points. For example, in the event that you're posting about another tech item, including industry-explicit hashtags like #TechInnovation or #GadgetLover can open your substance to a more extensive crowd past your nearby devotees.

In any case, the key is balance. While utilizing famous hashtags expands your range, depending entirely on them could suffocate your substance in an ocean of posts. Consolidating specialty or marked hashtags can assist with keeping an equilibrium, guaranteeing your substance contacts the right crowd. In addition to being your brand's signature, these distinctive hashtags help to build communities. Your online presence will grow and your audience will feel more connected if they are encouraged to use your brand's hashtag when sharing content.

Taking advantage of latest things is similarly urgent. Trending topics or challenges are frequently accompanied by dedicated hashtags on social media platforms. Your visibility and engagement could soar dramatically if you take part in these trends. It exhibits your image's significance and versatility to current discussions, adjusting your substance to what's catching the web-based local area's consideration.

Nonetheless, realness is key while bouncing on patterns. Participation that is forced or irrelevant can backfire, resulting in a disconnect with your audience. Prior to joining a pattern, evaluate its arrangement with your image personality and values. Make content that flawlessly incorporates the pattern into your story as opposed to feeling like a constrained endeavor to ride the wave.

When using hashtags and trends, it is essential to monitor social media analytics. Data-driven adjustments are made possible by insights into which trends and hashtags are attracting your audience's attention and driving engagement. Analytics tools that show impressions, reach, and engagement metrics related to your posts are frequently provided by platforms. Consistently breaking down this information refines your hashtag methodology and guarantees you stay receptive to your crowd's inclinations.

A branded hashtag campaign can also revolutionize the industry. Laying out a one of a kind hashtag intended for your showcasing effort supports client produced content, encouraging a feeling of local area around your image. In addition to increasing engagement, this provides a steady supply of genuine content that can be utilized in subsequent marketing campaigns.

Another effective tactic is collaborating with industry influencers. A hashtag campaign's reach can be exponentially increased through the participation or endorsement of influential people, who typically have a large and dedicated following. Look for influencers whose followers are similar to the people you want to reach and think about forming partnerships with them that will benefit both of you and leverage their authority.

A successful social media strategy relies heavily on trends and hashtags. Utilizing hashtags effectively increases discoverability, and embracing current trends demonstrates your brand's adaptability and relevance. Finding some kind of harmony among well known and specialty hashtags, partaking truly in patterns, and bridling examination for nonstop improvement are fundamental strategies in the powerful universe of virtual entertainment promoting.

You can ultimately increase your brand's visibility, engage a larger audience, and stay ahead of the curve in the ever-changing digital landscape by mastering the art of leveraging hashtags and trends.

# Chapter 4
# Email Marketing for the Holidays

Email showcasing during special times of year is a pivotal procedure for organizations hoping to gain by the happy season and lift their deals. The Christmas season furnishes a novel chance to interface with clients, construct brand dependability, and drive income through compelling email crusades. In this article, we will investigate the vital components of effective occasion email promoting and give tips to making significant missions.

## 1. Begin Early and Plan Ahead:

Early planning is essential to the success of holiday email marketing. Advertisers ought to begin arranging their vacation email crusades well ahead of time to guarantee a consistent and top notch procedure. This includes crafting compelling content and establishing goals and target audiences. Businesses can avoid the rush at the last minute and create a cohesive series of emails that resonate with their audience by starting early.

## 2. Create a festive email layout:

The visual allure of occasion messages is essential for catching the consideration of beneficiaries. Consolidating happy and occasional plans makes a bright and drawing air. This incorporates utilizing occasion themed illustrations, tones, and symbolism that line up with the brand. An outwardly engaging email is bound to hang out in swarmed inboxes and urge beneficiaries to investigate the substance.

## 3. Divide Your Email Lists:

Division is a useful asset in email promoting, and during special times of year, it turns out to be much more basic. Organizations ought to fragment their email records in view of variables like buy history, inclinations, and socioeconomics. This considers customized and designated correspondence, guaranteeing that beneficiaries get significant substance that reverberates with their inclinations. Personalization upgrades the general client experience and improves the probability of changes.

**4. Make compelling content:**

The composed substance of occasion messages ought to be convincing, brief, and lined up with the brand's voice. Create messages that bring out the occasion soul and reverberate with the feelings of the time. Feature exceptional advancements, selective offers, and restricted time arrangements to make a need to get a move on among beneficiaries. Recipients are encouraged to take action by clear and persuasive copy, whether that action is making a purchase, signing up for a newsletter, or engaging with the brand on social media.

**5. Offer Special Offers and Discounts:**

One of the vital drivers of occasion email advertising achievement is offering select arrangements and advancements. Clients are effectively searching for limits and exceptional proposals during the Christmas season, making it a helpful time for organizations to grandstand their best arrangements. Think about running restricted time advancements, streak deals, or elite limits for email supporters of boost buys and reward client steadfastness.

**6. Put responsive design into action:**

With the rising utilization of cell phones, it's fundamental to guarantee that occasion messages are improved for different screen sizes. Carrying out a responsive plan guarantees that messages look engaging and are not difficult to explore on both work areas and cell phones. A consistent client experience across various gadgets adds to higher open rates, navigate rates, and by and large mission achievement.

## 7. Influence Robotization:

Email marketing campaigns during the holiday season can greatly benefit from automation. Set up computerized work processes for welcome messages, truck surrender updates, and post-buy subsequent meet-ups. Businesses can save time and money and maintain a consistent communication flow throughout the holiday season thanks to automation, which enables them to send messages that are timely and pertinent without the need for human intervention.

## 8. Make yourself feel urgent:

The Christmas season is described by a need to get a move on, with clients effectively looking for convenient presents and advancements. In holiday emails, use persuasive language and countdown timers to elicit a sense of urgency. Featuring restricted time offers or underlining the oncoming occasion cutoff times can inspire beneficiaries to make a quick move, driving transformations and expanding the effect of the mission.

## 9. Analyze and Monitor Performance:

Utilize analytics and key performance indicators (KPIs) on a regular basis to keep an eye on how well holiday email campaigns are performing. Keep track of metrics like click-through rates, open rates, conversion rates, and revenue generated. Dissecting effort information gives important experiences into what procedures are working and where changes might be required. Make use of this data to improve the efficiency of your email marketing efforts and optimize future campaigns.

**10. Cultivate Client Commitment:**

Holiday email marketing offers a chance to cultivate customer engagement and establish long-term relationships in addition to increasing sales. Utilizing user-generated content, social media engagement, or feedback surveys, encourage recipients to share their holiday experiences with the brand. Building a feeling of local area and association can add to long haul client steadfastness and brand support.

All in all, occasion email promoting is an incredible asset for organizations to associate with their crowd, drive deals, and construct brand steadfastness during the bubbly season. By beginning early, arranging in an intelligent way, and integrating these critical components into their missions, advertisers can make effective and paramount occasion email encounters that reverberate with beneficiaries and add to generally speaking business achievement.

# Crafting Festive Email Campaigns

Businesses use creative and strategic methods to connect with their audience on special occasions by creating festive email campaigns. A well-executed email campaign can be a powerful tool for building brand loyalty, driving sales, and fostering a positive relationship with customers during the holiday season, the New Year, or any other festive event.

**Understanding the Spirit of the Season:**

To make a fruitful merry email crusade, understanding the soul of the occasion is vital. Themes and emotions evoked by various festivals vary. For instance, while New Year's celebrations center on reflection, resolutions, and fresh beginnings, the holiday season frequently places an emphasis on warmth, joy, and family. Fitting your email content to reverberate with these subjects makes a more significant association with your crowd.

**Personalization through segmentation:**

When it comes to festive email campaigns, no one size fits all. Your messages can be tailored based on demographics, preferences, and purchase history using customer segmentation. Beyond simply addressing recipients by their first names, personalization includes conveying content that reverberates with their inclinations and necessities. You can send targeted offers and recommendations by segmenting your audience, which increases engagement and conversion rates.

**Eye-Getting Plan and Symbolism:**

Visual allure assumes an essential part in getting the notice of your crowd. Merry email crusades give a chance to imbue innovativeness into your plans. Think about using graphics with the celebration's theme, festive imagery, and vibrant colors. Notwithstanding, guarantee that the plan stays predictable with your image personality to keep an expert and strong look.

**Attractive Subject Lines:**

The headline is the doorway to your email. Create compelling subject lines that pique recipients' curiosity and encourage them to open your email. Integrate happy components and a need to get going, for example, restricted time offers or selective arrangements, to support prompt activity. A well-written subject line increases engagement and sets the tone for the entire email.

**Connecting with Content:**

When your email is opened, the substance should satisfy the commitment of the title. Foster drawing in and applicable substance that lines up with the happy topic. The recipient's festive experience can be enhanced by sharing stories, highlighting special promotions, or providing useful content. A sense of community around your brand can also be created by including testimonials or user-generated content.

**Versatile Responsiveness:**

It is a non-negotiable requirement for your festive email campaigns to be mobile-responsive in an era when a significant portion of email opens occur on mobile devices. Streamline pictures and designs for more modest screens, and test your messages across different gadgets and email clients to ensure a consistent client experience. High bounce rates and missed opportunities can result from an email that is poorly optimized.

**Clear CTA (call to action):**

Each happy email ought to have an unmistakable and convincing source of inspiration. The call to action (CTA) should be prominent and persuasive, whether it is directing recipients to a special holiday promotion, encouraging them to explore new collections, or inviting them to participate in a contest with a festive theme. Utilize noteworthy language that spurs beneficiaries to make the ideal next strides.

**Virtual Entertainment Joining:**

Broaden the scope of your bubbly email crusades by incorporating online entertainment components. Recipients should be encouraged to share festive promotions or user-generated content on social media. Counting virtual entertainment fastens or connects in your messages empowers simple sharing, enhancing the effect of your mission and encouraging local area commitment.

**Investigation and Emphasis:**

For determining whether or not your festive email campaign was successful, post-campaign analytics are essential. Keep an eye on important metrics like click-through, open, and conversion rates. Analyze customer behavior to learn what worked well and what might need to be improved. Utilize these insights to iterate and improve your festive campaign strategies.

All in all, making bubbly email crusades requires a smart mix of imagination, personalization, and key preparation. You can create memorable and successful campaigns that resonate with your customers by comprehending the spirit of the occasion, segmenting your audience, employing eye-catching design, delivering engaging content, and so on. Analytics-based optimization ensures that your subsequent festive email campaigns build on previous successes and cultivate long-term connections with your audience.

# Timing and Frequency Considerations

From electronics and telecommunications to music and everyday activities, timing and frequency considerations are important in many areas. Understanding and dealing with these viewpoints is fundamental for guaranteeing the legitimate working of frameworks and gadgets, as well as upgrading execution.

In the domain of gadgets and computerized frameworks, timing alludes to the exact coordination of occasions or signals. Whether it's a PC processor executing directions, a memory module getting to information, or a correspondence framework communicating data, exact timing is indispensable for precise and dependable activity. Timing considerations are crucial in digital circuits to avoid problems like data corruption, signal interference, or synchronization errors.

Recurrence, then again, is a proportion of how frequently a rehashing occasion happens per unit of time. Frequency is frequently associated with a processor's clock speed or the rate at which data is transmitted in the field of electronics. While faster processing and communication are generally possible with higher frequencies, there are downsides such as increased power consumption and the possibility of signal integrity issues.

One of the critical ideas in timing and recurrence contemplations is the clock signal. A clock signal is used as a metronome in digital systems to control the speed of operations. The clock's recurrence decides the speed of these tasks, and synchronized timing guarantees that various parts of a framework cooperate consistently. Errors and decreased performance can result from timing deviations, or jitter. Designs fastidiously plan and examine timing outlines to limit jitter and advance framework execution.

In broadcast communications, timing is basic for guaranteeing exact information transmission. In network correspondences, synchronization between gadgets is fundamental to stay away from information crashes and parcel misfortune. In high-speed communication systems like 5G networks, where precise timing is required to maintain low latency and high data throughput, timing considerations become even more important.

Past the domain of innovation, timing assumes a huge part in music and human expression. Timing is what musicians use to make rhythm, harmony, and melody. A very much planned presentation improves the profound effect of music, showing the significance of timing in the computerized domain as well as in the imaginative expressions.

In daily existence, timing impacts different parts of our schedules. Effective time management requires an understanding of timing and synchronization for everything from bus travel to meal preparation. Efficiency and productivity increase as a whole when tasks and activities are coordinated effectively and on time.

The natural world is also subject to frequency considerations. The idea of frequency is used in physics to describe things like sound waves and electromagnetic radiation. The recurrence of a sound wave decides its pitch, while in the electromagnetic range, various frequencies compare to various sorts of radiation, from radio waves to gamma beams.

Diagnostic procedures and treatment plans in the medical field must take into account timing and frequency. In clinical imaging, exact timing is fundamental for catching clear and precise pictures. When taking medications, ensuring that prescribed dosages are taken at specific intervals reduces the likelihood of side effects and maximizes effectiveness.

Our capacity to measure time with an unprecedented level of precision has been revolutionized by the development of technologies like atomic clocks. Nuclear tickers utilize the vibrations of molecules as a source of perspective, giving profoundly exact timekeeping. The synchronization of these nuclear tickers is significant for applications like worldwide route frameworks (GPS), where exact timing is fundamental for deciding area arranges.

Taking everything into account, timing and recurrence contemplations are unavoidable across different disciplines, affecting the plan of electronic frameworks, the exhibition of media communications organizations, the production of music and workmanship, and, surprisingly, the working of ordinary exercises. A nuanced understanding of timing and frequency is necessary for achieving precision, efficiency, and dependability in a variety of applications, whether in the field of technology, the arts, or natural phenomena.

# Chapter 5
# Optimizing Website and Landing Pages

Upgrading sites and greeting pages is pivotal for making on the web progress. In the present computerized age, where capacities to focus are short and contests are wild, a very much upgraded site can have the effect between drawing in guests and losing them to contenders. This streamlining system includes a blend of specialized, plan, and content-related procedures pointed toward improving client experience, supporting web crawler perceivability, and at last driving transformations.

**1. Responsive Plan:**

Verify the mobile friendliness of your website and landing pages.A responsive design is essential for providing a seamless user experience across various devices in light of the growing use of smartphones. Google additionally focuses on versatile sites in its hunt rankings.

**2. Page Speed Enhancement:**
For a website to keep visitors, it must load quickly. Slow-stacking pages can prompt high skip rates and adversely influence web index rankings. Pack pictures, minify code, and influence program storing to enhance page stacking times. Google PageSpeed Insights and other similar tools can help you understand where you can make improvements.

**3. Watchword Exploration and Web optimization:**
Lead intensive watchword examination to comprehend what your interest group is looking for. Include relevant keywords naturally in the content, meta tags, and headers of your website. Create a solid SEO strategy to boost your website's visibility in search results and bring in organic visitors.

**4. Clear Source of inspiration (CTA):**
A convincing and clear CTA guides guests on what move to make straightaway. Whether it's making a buy, pursuing a bulletin, or reaching your group, decisively place CTAs all through your site and greeting pages. Utilize differentiating colors and influential language to make them stick out.

**5. Relevant and Engaging Content:**
Quality substance is the foundation of any effective site. Make content that tends to the requirements and interests

of your interest group. Utilize a blend of text, visuals, and media components to make your substance locking in. Keep your content current on a regular basis to stay relevant and demonstrate your industry expertise.

**6. A/B Testing:**
Try different things with various components on your greeting pages through A/B testing. Test varieties of titles, CTA buttons, pictures, and different components to recognize what reverberates best with your crowd. Use information driven experiences to refine your pages for ideal execution.

**7. Easy to understand Route:**
Improve the on site route to guarantee guests can undoubtedly find what they're searching for. A positive user experience is made possible by clear categories, intuitive menus, and a logical site structure. The objective is to limit the quantity of snaps it takes for clients to arrive at their ideal objective.

**8. Social Evidence:**
Integrate social confirmation components, like client tributes, surveys, or contextual analyses, to fabricate trust and believability. Your brand's reputation can be improved and potential buyers influenced by positive feedback from satisfied customers.

**9. Improve Pictures and Media:**
Enhance pictures and mixed media components to further develop page stacking times without compromising quality. Utilize compacted picture designs, execute sluggish stacking for pictures beneath the crease, and guarantee recordings are facilitated on solid stages for consistent playback.

## 10. Examination and Information Following:

Execute examination devices, for example, Google Investigation to follow client conduct on your site. Understand user interactions, identify popular content, and potential areas for improvement by analyzing data. This data is significant for going with information driven choices to enhance your site further.

## 11. Security:

Guarantee your site has powerful safety efforts set up. A solid site safeguards client information as well as adds to higher web index rankings. Monitor for any potential vulnerabilities, regularly update software, and install SSL certificates.

## 12. Neighborhood Improvement:

In the event that your business has an actual area, upgrade your site for neighborhood look. Make sure your address, phone number, and business hours are correct, include local keywords, and claim and verify your Google My Business listing.

All in all, upgrading sites and presentation pages is a continuous cycle that requires a diverse methodology. By zeroing in on responsive plan, page speed, Web optimization, convincing substance, and client experience, you can make a site that draws in guests as well as converts them into faithful clients. Consistently screen examination, remain refreshed on industry drifts, and adjust your improvement systems to remain ahead in the unique web-based scene.

# Decorating Your Online Presence

It's like decorating a room—everything adds to the overall atmosphere—to create an appealing and effective online presence. The way you present yourself online can have a significant impact on how people view you as an individual, a company, or a brand. Let's take a look at some important aspects of decorating your online space to make it inviting, real, and memorable.

**1. Design:** The Groundwork of Your Computerized Space Similarly as a very much planned room establishes the vibe for a happy with living space, a nicely planned site or web-based entertainment profile lays out the underpinning of your internet based presence. Choose a layout that is simple and easy to use, and use fonts and a color scheme that are consistent with your personality or brand identity. To ensure a smooth user experience, strike a balance between aesthetics and functionality.

**2. Content:** The Work of art of Your Web-based Material Quality substance is the work of art that beautifies your computerized material. Whether it's blog entries, recordings, or online entertainment refreshes, guarantee that your substance is important, connecting with, and enhances your crowd. Tailor your informing to reverberate with your ideal interest group, and keep up with consistency in tone across stages. Consider each piece of content to be a brushstroke that adds to the finished piece.

**3. Authenticity:** The Individual Touch
Similarly as an individual touch can cause an actual space to feel warm and inviting, inject your web-based presence with genuineness. To truly connect with your audience, share your story, your experiences, and your values. Legitimacy constructs trust and encourages a feeling of local area, making individuals bound to draw in with and support your web-based tries.

**4. The Internet:** The Social Media Hub
Your online presence's bustling hubs are the social media platforms. Improve these spaces with standard updates, intuitive substance, and significant discussions. Pick stages that line up with your objectives and interest group. Draw in with your supporters, answer remarks, and exhibit your character. Virtual entertainment isn't simply a special device; it's a space for building connections.

**5. Photography:** The Visual Elegance
The pieces of art that make your online space look better are high-quality images. Put resources into proficient photography or utilize outwardly engaging stock pictures. A cohesive aesthetic is achieved by using imagery that is consistent across your website and social media platforms. Visuals are strong — they catch consideration and pass on messages immediately, so guarantee they line up with your image or individual style.

**6. Navigation:** The Pathways in Your Advanced Home Simple route is what might be compared to very much arranged pathways in an actual space.

Guarantee that guests can without much of a stretch find what they're searching for on your site. Smooth out menus, utilize clear suggestions to take action, and streamline for cell phones. A user-friendly interface prevents frustration and bounce-backs by encouraging exploration and keeping visitors engaged.

**7. Storytelling:** The Narrative Thread You can incorporate storytelling into your online presence in the same way that storytelling creates a narrative thread throughout a physical space. Share convincing stories that reverberate with your crowd, whether it's the excursion of your business, individual accounts, or client tributes. Narrating makes profound associations, making your web-based presence paramount.

**8. Consistency:** The String that Ties Everything Together Consistency is the string that ties every one of the components of your web-based presence together. From marking components to posting plans, keep a reliable picture. This aides in laying out a conspicuous personality, building trust, and cultivating a feeling of dependability. Your audience will have a seamless experience if you are consistent across platforms.

**9. Accessibility:** Inviting Everybody In Similarly as a genuinely open space is inviting to all, guarantee that your internet based presence is open. Make your content readable for all users, provide alternative text for images, and optimize your website for accessibility standards. A comprehensive web-based space shows a guarantee to contacting a different crowd.

**10.  Analytics:** The Input CircleExamination go about as the criticism circle in your advanced adorning venture. Analytical data should be reviewed on a regular basis to determine what is working well and what needs to be improved. Track site traffic, commitment measurements, and virtual entertainment examination. Make use of this data to improve your strategy by concentrating on the aspects that have the greatest impact on your audience.

you need to carefully combine design, content, authenticity, and engagement when decorating your online presence. Similarly as a very much designed room mirrors the character of its occupant, an insightfully arranged web-based space grandstands your personality or brand. Routinely update and invigorate your computerized stylistic layout to remain significant and keep a powerful internet based presence that enamors and interfaces with your crowd.

# Streamlining the Purchase Process

Smoothing out the buy cycle is an urgent part of current business tasks, intending to upgrade productivity, diminish costs, and further develop generally speaking consumer loyalty. Organizations are constantly looking for ways to simplify and speed up the process of selecting products and completing transactions in today's fast-paced digital environment.

Utilizing cutting-edge technology is one of the most important factors in streamlining the purchasing process. Customers will have a smooth online shopping experience if e-commerce platforms are put in place that are easy to use. These stages ought to be planned with an emphasis on instinctive route, clear item data, and a direct checkout process. Incorporating secure installment doors adds an additional layer of comfort and trust, working with a quick and secure exchange.

Besides, the consolidation of man-made consciousness (artificial intelligence) and AI can assume a significant part in smoothing out the buy venture. Artificial intelligence controlled chatbots, for example, can give continuous help to clients, noting questions, and directing them through the determination and buying process. The behavior and preferences of customers can be analyzed by machine learning algorithms, which then provide customized product recommendations that enhance the shopping experience as a whole.

In addition to advancements in technology, efficient communication is crucial to streamlining the purchasing process. Customers are able to quickly make decisions that are based on accurate information when product descriptions are both concise and high-quality. Transparent pricing and shipping information ought to be simple to find, eliminating any ambiguity that might prevent a customer from making a purchase.

Carrying out a hearty stock administration framework is one more vital part of a proficient buy process. Constant following of item accessibility keeps clients from encountering disillusionment because of unavailable things. This smoothes out the buy interaction as well as adds to consumer loyalty and dependability.

Moreover, coordinated effort with solid providers is fundamental in keeping a smooth and proficient production network. Strong partnerships reduce the likelihood of delays or disruptions by ensuring a consistent supply of high-quality goods. By streamlining the production network, associations can limit lead times and improve by and large functional productivity.

In order to continuously improve the purchasing procedure, invaluable tools like customer feedback and data analysis are utilized. Gathering criticism on the whole purchasing venture distinguishes trouble spots and regions that require improvement. Businesses can adapt and tailor their strategies to meet changing consumer preferences by analyzing customer data for trends.

To smooth out the buy interaction really, organizations should focus on portable enhancement. With the rising pervasiveness of cell phones, a dynamic buying experience is non-debatable. On mobile devices, a streamlined and effective transaction process is made possible by responsive design, quick loading times, and user-friendly interfaces.

Notwithstanding innovation and correspondence upgrades, a smoothed out buy process requires an essential way to deal with client relationships with the executives (CRM). Constructing and keeping an exhaustive client data set empowers organizations to customize communications, expect needs, and give a more custom-made shopping experience. This, thus, adds to consumer loyalty and rehash business.

While zeroing in on proficiency, thinking twice about security is vital now. Executing powerful network safety measures safeguards client information and monetary data, cultivating trust and trust in the buy cycle. Security elements, for example, encryption, secure attachments layer (SSL) testaments, and two-factor validation are fundamental parts of a solid internet based exchange climate.

All in all, smoothing out the buy cycle is a multi-layered effort that requires a mix of cutting edge innovation, viable correspondence, vital organizations, and a pledge to persistent improvement. By utilizing the force of innovation, upgrading supply chains, focusing on client experience, and guaranteeing security, organizations can make a buy cycle that isn't just proficient yet additionally improves consumer loyalty and faithfulness in the quickly developing scene of present day business.

# Chapter 6
# Partnerships
# and

# Collaboration s

Organizations and coordinated efforts assume a urgent part in encouraging development, driving development, and accomplishing shared objectives across different enterprises. The synergy created by strategic alliances frequently produces outcomes that surpass individual efforts, regardless of whether they are in the nonprofit, academic, or business sectors.

In this investigation of organizations and coordinated efforts, we'll dig into their importance, key components for progress, and the advancing scene of cooperative undertakings.

**The Importance of Collaborations:**

Organizations are able to navigate complexities and take advantage of collective capabilities thanks to partnerships, which provide a means of leveraging complementary strengths and resources. In the business domain, vital collisions between organizations can upgrade market presence, smooth out tasks, and speed up item improvement. By pooling skill and sharing dangers, accomplices can defeat difficulties that may be unconquerable all alone.

Additionally, academic and research collaborations increase the likelihood of groundbreaking discoveries and advancements. Experts from a variety of fields work together in cross-disciplinary collaborations to foster an atmosphere where innovative concepts and interdisciplinary solutions emerge.

These associations contribute not exclusively to the development of individual associations yet in addition to the advancement of whole businesses.

In the not-for-profit area, joint efforts are instrumental in resolving complex social issues. Partnerships are often formed by nonprofit organizations to pool resources, share best practices, and increase their impact. These coalitions make an organization impact, empowering charities to successfully contact more extensive crowds and address fundamental difficulties more.

**Important Components of a Successful Collaboration:**

Fruitful organizations rely on a groundwork of clear correspondence, shared values, and common advantage. From the beginning, it is essential to have a common understanding of goals and expectations. A distinct understanding framing each accomplice's jobs, obligations, and commitments evades misconceptions and guarantees arrangement all through the cooperation.

The foundation of successful partnerships is trust. Transparency, dependability, and a dedication to common goals are necessary for establishing and maintaining trust. Ordinary correspondence and criticism systems assume a vital part in sustaining trust among accomplices, cultivating a climate where everybody feels esteemed and heard.

Adaptability is one more key component in fruitful coordinated efforts. The business scene is dynamic, and unanticipated difficulties might emerge. Over time, partnerships that are able to change with the times and pivot when necessary are more likely to last and succeed.

Social arrangement is frequently misjudged however is vital, particularly in worldwide joint efforts. Understanding and regarding the social subtleties of each accomplice association add to an amicable working relationship and relieve likely struggles.

In environments that foster collaboration and welcome a variety of points of view, innovation thrives. Associations ought to advance a comprehensive culture that esteems the one of a kind commitments of every member. This variety improves imagination as well as results in additional hearty answers for complex issues.

## The Changing Landscape of Cooperative Projects:

In the computerized age, innovation has turned into an impetus for new types of coordinated effort. Cloud computing, data-sharing platforms, and virtual collaboration tools have made it easier for partners to collaborate across borders.

Distant cooperation has become progressively common, permitting associations to take advantage of worldwide ability pools and work consistently across time regions.

In addition, the way businesses approach collaboration has changed as a result of the rise of open innovation. Open development includes looking for outside thoughts, advancements, and mastery to supplement inner capacities.

Organizations can speed up innovation cycles and remain at the forefront of their respective industries by embracing external contributions.

PPPs, or public-private partnerships, have emerged as a popular model for addressing societal issues. Legislatures, organizations, and philanthropies team up to use every area's assets in drives going from foundation advancement to medical care.

PPPs achieve lasting results by combining the efficiency of the private sector with the social responsibility of the public sector.

All in all, associations and coordinated efforts are essential systems for driving advancement and accomplishing shared goals. Whether in business, the scholarly community, or the philanthropic area, the collaboration made through essential collusions improves development, enhances influence, and adds to the aggregate headway of society.

As the scene keeps on developing, associations that embrace coordinated effort as an essential basic are ready to flourish in an interconnected and quickly impacting world.

# Collaborative Marketing Opportunities

Cooperative promoting open doors present organizations with inventive ways of intensifying their compass, improve brand perceivability, and cultivate commonly valuable connections. In a period where rivalry is wild and customer consideration is momentary, working together with different organizations can be an essential move that yields great outcomes. A platform for shared success is provided by this strategy, which involves joint efforts in planning, executing, and promoting marketing initiatives.

At the core of cooperative advertising is the collaboration gotten from pooling assets, ability, and crowds. Partnerships and joint ventures are a common method of collaboration. By lining up with correlative organizations, organizations can take advantage of one another's assets and influence aggregate capacities. For instance, a wellness clothing brand could team up with a wellbeing application to offer elite limits or make co-marked content that resounds with wellbeing cognizant customers.

Co-marketing campaigns are another way to collaborate in marketing. This involves the collaboration of two or more brands to promote a service or product. Co-marketing allows businesses to share the costs of marketing campaigns in addition to expanding the promotional reach. When technology companies work with software developers to show how their products seamlessly integrate with one another to provide users with a more complete solution, this is a great example.

Virtual entertainment, a force to be reckoned with in contemporary promoting, offers plentiful open doors for cooperation. Brands can cross-advance each other's substance, participate in joint giveaways, or even host Instagram takeovers. Such drives acquaint each brand with different devotees, extending the potential client base. For example, a style brand and a marvel brand could team up on a virtual entertainment challenge where clients are urged to make looks consolidating both design and magnificence components.

Businesses of similar sizes and industries are not excluded from collaborative marketing. As a matter of fact, probably the best coordinated efforts rise up out of organizations between apparently divergent elements. A high-end fashion brand's partnership with a fast food chain is one example. By mixing extravagance with daily existence, the two brands can contact new crowds and make essential, shareable substance that flashes discussions.

Collaboration has also become a powerful strategy in influencer marketing. To amplify their message, brands can engage multiple influencers simultaneously. Working together with powerhouses who share a comparable interest group guarantees a more durable and effective mission. A tech organization could team up with a gathering of educated powerhouses to make genuine substance displaying the commonsense uses of their items in regular daily existence.

Furthermore, collaboration within an organization is a part of collaborative marketing as well as partnerships with external partners. To ensure a seamless and comprehensive customer experience, various departments, including marketing, sales, and customer service, can work together. A marketing team might, for instance, work with the customer service team to make content that answers common questions from customers. This would show that the company cares about making sure its customers are happy.

A nuanced approach is required for measuring the success of collaborative marketing efforts. In addition to traditional metrics like reach and engagement, key performance indicators (KPIs) may also include new customer acquisition and brand perception. Following the effect on deals and brand feeling evaluates the substantial results of cooperative drives, giving significant bits of knowledge to future undertakings.

All in all, cooperatives promoting valuable open doors are a dynamic and successful way for organizations to explore the intricacies of the cutting edge market. By uniting with different substances, whether through associations, co-showcasing efforts, web-based entertainment coordinated efforts, or powerhouse organizations, organizations can take advantage of new crowds, share assets, and make significant missions that leave an enduring effect. Collaborative marketing is a strategic pillar for brands aiming to thrive in a competitive landscape in an interconnected world where consumers seek authenticity and meaningful connections.

# Cross-Promotions with Other Businesses

A strategic and mutually beneficial strategy for increasing brand awareness, extending customer reach, and driving sales can be cross-promotions with other businesses. Through well-executed cross-promotional campaigns, businesses can capitalize on each other's strengths in a world where collaboration frequently results in innovation and success.

At its center, cross-advancement includes at least two organizations meeting up to advance each other's items or administrations. This collaboration can take a variety of forms, including joint marketing campaigns, products branded together, events shared, and even promotions that are reciprocal. The key is to distinguish accomplices whose ideal interest group lines up with your own, making a collaboration that improves the general effect of the special endeavors.

The capacity to acquire new customers is one of the primary benefits of cross-promotions. By collaborating with a business that takes special care of a comparable segment yet offers corresponding items or administrations, the two players can arrive at potential clients who probably won't have been presented to their image in any case. For instance, a fitness equipment manufacturer and a fitness apparel brand might work together to reach a broader audience interested in a healthy and active lifestyle.

Additionally, cross-promotions may offer low-cost marketing options. Sharing the costs of a showcasing effort, occasion, or publicizing materials can fundamentally diminish the monetary weight on every business included. This permits more modest organizations, specifically, to get to showcasing channels and open doors that could have been generally unattainable. By pooling assets, the two players can make a more significant and effective special presence.

Besides, cross-advancements can improve validity and trust among shoppers. A sense of endorsement is created when two reputable businesses align their brands. Purchasers are bound to trust and draw in with an item or administration when it comes suggested by a brand they as of now trust. This trust move can prompt expanded changes and long haul client unwaveringly, helping both teaming up organizations simultaneously.

To guarantee the outcome of a cross-limited time crusade, laying out clear targets and assumptions from the very start is pivotal. Characterize the objectives of the cooperation, whether they are centered around expanding deals, growing business sector reach, or fortifying brand picture. The campaign's planning and execution will be guided by a shared understanding of the desired outcomes, ensuring that both parties are working toward mutually beneficial outcomes.

Another important aspect of successful cross-promotions is efficient communication between businesses that collaborate. From adjusting on the mission's information to planning strategies and courses of events, open and straightforward correspondence is fundamental. Customary registrations and updates assist with forestalling false impressions and guarantee that the two players are in total agreement all through the special period.

Choosing the right accomplice is basic for the progress of a cross-advancement. Preferably, organizations ought to look for accomplices that share comparable qualities, target socioeconomics, and in general brand similarity. A misalignment here can weaken the viability of the mission and may try and have negative repercussions on the brands in question. To ensure a strategic fit, any collaboration should be preceded by thorough research and due diligence.

All in all, cross-advancements with different organizations offer a plenty of advantages, going from extended client reach and financially savvy promoting to expanded believability and trust. By decisively lining up with viable accomplices, setting clear targets, and cultivating open correspondence, organizations can open the maximum capacity of cross-limited time crusades. Collaboration continues to be a powerful tool for those who want to succeed in a competitive market, even as the business landscape continues to change.

# Chapter 7 Customer Retention Strategies

Retaining current customers is essential to the success of any business. While drawing in new clients is fundamental, keeping a dedicated client base can essentially influence long haul benefit. Executing viable client maintenance systems is vital to accomplishing this objective.

One principal procedure is to give remarkable client support.Feeling respected and supported by a brand increases the likelihood that customers will continue with it.This includes tending to client requests instantly, settling issues effectively, and going above and beyond to surpass assumptions. Customers have a positive experience and become more loyal to businesses that place a high value on customer service.

Building solid associations with clients is one more essential part of maintenance. Personalization is an amazing asset in such a manner. Businesses can make customers feel more connected and appreciated by comprehending their preferences and tailoring interactions accordingly. This could be in the form of individualized                    product recommendations, individualized communication, or exclusive offers based on an individual's purchasing habits.

A well-liked and efficient strategy for encouraging repeat business is the use of loyalty programs. Offering prizes, limits, or select admittance to faithful clients boosts them to proceed with their support as well as causes them to feel recognized and esteemed. The construction of dedication projects can shift, from direct based frameworks toward layered participations, contingent upon the idea of the business.

Customer retention necessitates regular communication. Whether through email pamphlets, online entertainment, or different channels, keeping in contact keeps the brand top-of-mind. Sharing updates, pertinent substance, and elite offers can build up the client's association with the brand and brief them to make rehash buys.

Gathering and utilizing client criticism is an important maintenance procedure. By effectively looking for and standing by listening to client feelings, organizations can recognize regions for development, address concerns, and improve the general client experience. Answering input, whether positive or negative, shows a promise to consumer loyalty and can transform a disappointed client into a dependable backer.

Delivering high-quality goods or services on a regular basis is an essential component of customer retention. Clients return when they trust a brand to meet or surpass their assumptions reliably. Reliability is built through consistency, which is essential for maintaining long-term relationships with customers.

Retention is greatly aided by providing a seamless and convenient customer experience. This entails making sure that customers can easily navigate and access the products or services they require, streamlining the purchasing process, and optimizing both online and offline touchpoints. A problem free encounter lessons grinding, making clients bound to return.

Web-based entertainment assumes an urgent part in current client maintenance systems. Drawing in with clients on stages they regularly permit organizations to fabricate a local area around their image. Answering remarks, sharing client created content, and effectively taking part in important discussions add to a positive brand picture and upgrade client faithfulness.

Shock and pleasure strategies can have an enduring effect on clients. Customers can be made to feel special and appreciated in a big way by providing them with unexpected perks, gifts, or personalized acts. This not only increases the likelihood of customers recommending the brand to others but also encourages repeat business.

For successful customer retention, a robust customer relationship management (CRM) system must be implemented. A CRM framework helps organizations coordinate and oversee client information, track communications, and designer promoting endeavors. Businesses can anticipate customer needs and preferences by utilizing data insights, allowing them to proactively address issues and provide customized solutions.

All in all, client maintenance is a diverse exertion that requires a mix of techniques zeroed in on giving remarkable encounters, building connections, and offering unmistakable impetuses. Focusing on consumer loyalty, personalization, and steady quality makes an establishment for long haul steadfastness. Organizations that put resources into thorough client maintenance procedures hold existing clients as well as advantage from positive verbal, expanded client lifetime esteem, and a feasible upper hand on the lookout.

# Loyalty Programs for the Holidays

During the holiday season, loyalty programs have an even greater impact on consumer behavior because of their central role in shaping consumer behavior. As businesses try to take advantage of the festive mood, these programs, which are meant to reward and keep customers coming back, take on a special significance. In this article, we'll investigate the elements of reliability programs during special times of year, analyzing how they impact purchaser decisions, cultivate brand faithfulness, and add to the general outcome of organizations.

Consumer spending rises during the holiday season as people look for gifts for loved ones and indulge in festive purchases. Unwaveringly programs influence this flood in action by offering custom-made motivators, selective limits, and customized rewards. These advantages serve not just as a way to draw in new clients yet additionally as a procedure to hold existing ones. The charm of extra advantages frequently prompts customers to remain faithful to a specific brand, encouraging a feeling of association that stretches out past the Christmas season.

The element of surprise and delight is one important aspect of loyalty programs during the holidays. To create a sense of urgency and excitement among their devoted customer base, brands use special promotions, limited-time offers, and exclusive access to new products in a strategic manner. Businesses align their loyalty programs with the joyful atmosphere of the season by designing these incentives with a holiday theme. This energizes expanded spending as well as has a positive and essential effect on clients.

During the holidays, personalization plays a crucial role in the success of loyalty programs. Loyalty programs with rewards that are tailored to each customer's preferences stand out in an era when customers are looking for more individualized shopping experiences.

Businesses can provide rewards that are not only pertinent but also meaningful by analyzing previous purchase behavior and comprehending customer preferences. This customized approach upgrades the client's general shopping experience, making a more profound close to home association with the brand.

Additionally, special times of year give an optimal open door to organizations to offer thanks to their dependable clients. To demonstrate a company's appreciation for its customers, loyalty programs can be designed with exclusive holiday-themed gifts, handwritten notes, or personalized messages.

This motion goes past conditional connections, cultivating a feeling of generosity and correspondence. Clients who feel esteemed are bound to stay faithful and may try and become brand advocates, spreading good informal exchange during the Christmas season.

During the holidays, loyalty programs can also benefit from integrating social media. Brands can urge clients to share their vacation buys, elite offers, and customized compensations on friendly stages. This fills in as free publicizing as well as makes a feeling of local area among steadfast clients. Client created content exhibiting occasion themed items or encounters further intensifies the brand's range and impact, adding to the general outcome of the unwaveringly program.

Loyalty programs emerge as a useful differentiation strategy for businesses as they navigate the fiercely competitive holiday marketing landscape. Offering interesting and captivating prizes separates a brand from its rivals, drawing in clients who are searching for quality items as well as for a customized and compensating shopping experience. The Christmas season fills in as a milestone for shopper consideration, and devotion programs arise as an essential weapon for organizations expecting to protect an enduring association with their crowd.

All in all, faithfulness programs employ huge impact during special times of year, furnishing organizations with an amazing asset to draw in, hold, and connect with clients. By consolidating shock and joy, personalization, appreciation, and web-based entertainment joining into their unwaveringly systems, brands can make an essential and compensating experience for their clients.

These programs have a lasting effect beyond the holiday season, laying the groundwork for customer advocacy and loyalty over time. Loyalty programs continue to be a key driver of success for businesses looking to succeed in the competitive holiday market as the holiday spirit continues to influence consumer behavior.

# Personalized Holiday Greetings

Customized occasion good tidings add an exceptional touch to the bubbly season, making significant associations and spreading bliss among companions, family, and partners. In a world immersed with nonexclusive messages, a redid welcoming sticks out, reflecting mindfulness and care. The individualization of messages, the acknowledgment of shared experiences, and the cultivation of a sense of warmth and belonging are just a few of the details that make personalized holiday greetings so appealing.

The recognition of one's individuality is at the heart of personalized holiday greetings. As opposed to sending an efficiently manufactured message that could undoubtedly be coordinated to anybody, getting some margin to make a hello that reverberates with the beneficiary's character, interests, or encounters raises the opinion. A connection develops that goes beyond the surface-level exchange of pleasantries when specific memories, shared experiences, or inside jokes are mentioned.

Personalization also shows that you really care about the relationship. It passes on the message that the source has given time and remembered to communicate their vacation wishes, causing the beneficiary to feel esteemed and appreciated. This deliberate effort is a testament to the relationship's strength and significance in a society where time is a scarce resource.

Beyond the written word, personalized holiday greetings go beyond words. In the advanced age, different stages offer open doors for customization, from making tailor made e-cards to sharing photograph arrangements catching the substance of shared minutes. Integrating visual components adds an additional layer of personalization, permitting people to exhibit their inventiveness and offer looks at their lives during the merry season.

Moreover, the effect of customized occasion good tidings reaches out to the working environment. In proficient settings, recognizing partners and clients with custom-made messages cultivates a positive corporate culture. It refines the business relationship, separating hindrances and making a more cooperative and harmonious climate. A touch of sincerity is added to the holiday wishes by recognizing individual achievements or milestones in the professional realm, thereby strengthening professional connections.

The growing significance of mindfulness and well-being is also aligned with the art of personalized greetings. Personalized holiday greetings offer a chance for genuine connection in a world where digital communication frequently lacks the depth of face-to-face interactions. These messages are an update that, even amidst occupied plans and innovative interruptions, individuals are carving out opportunity to interface on an individual level, cultivating a feeling of local area and backing.

In the domain of family and dear companionships, customized good tidings become esteemed tokens. The effort put into tailoring the greeting amplifies the emotional impact, whether through handwritten letters, carefully curated gift packages, or personalized video messages. These acts become symbols of enduring bonds and shared history in addition to holiday traditions.

Personalization is now easier than ever to achieve thanks to technological advancements. People can use a variety of resources to make their holiday greetings truly one-of-a-kind, such as templates that can be customized and tools powered by artificial intelligence that suggest content that is personalized. While the simplicity of computerized correspondence has prompted a wealth of messages during the Christmas season, the ones that stand apart are those injected with an individual touch.

Nonetheless, in the midst of the excitement for customized good tidings, finding some kind of harmony is fundamental. The expectation behind customization ought to be to improve the association, not to eclipse the pith of the occasion soul. Excessively intricate personalization can in some cases seem to be constrained or devious. Finding the sweet spot where the message feels genuine and sincere and reflects the sender's true feelings is the key.

All in all, customized occasion good tidings are a significant and effective method for praising the bubbly season. Whether divided between family, companions, or partners, these modified messages go past the normal, making enduring associations and cultivating a feeling of delight, warmth, and appreciation. As we explore the computerized scene of correspondence, the specialty of personalization turns into an incredible asset in spreading seasonal joy and fortifying the texture of our connections.

# Chapter 8
# Measuring
# Success

Estimating achievement is a nuanced and complex undertaking that stretches out across different parts of life, going from individual accomplishments to proficient achievements. It is a subjective and dynamic concept because the criteria for success can vary widely among individuals, cultures, and contexts. Whether in the domains of vocation, connections, or self-awareness, the measurements used to check a positive outcome frequently reflect individual qualities, cultural standards, and developing goals.

In the expert circle, achievement is much of the time measured through customary measurements like monetary profit, professional success, and expert acknowledgment. Income levels, net worth, and investment returns are common indicators of financial success. Although these metrics provide tangible indicators of prosperity, they frequently overlook less tangible aspects like job satisfaction and personal fulfillment.

Professional success is one more measuring stick for progress, with advancements, expanded liabilities, and positions of authority filling in as markers of expert accomplishment. Be that as it may, this viewpoint can disregard the significance of self-improvement, work fulfillment, and the general prosperity of people in their quest for progress. Modern conceptions of success are broadening to include a holistic perspective that places equal importance on professional accomplishments, mental health, work-life balance, and personal fulfillment.

Acknowledgment and approval inside one's expert field likewise add to the estimation of achievement. Grants, honors, and positive criticism from friends and bosses confirm the effect of a singular's commitments. However, achievement isn't exclusively reliant upon outer approval; In order to maintain achievement and contentment over the long term, intrinsic motivation and a sense of purpose are essential.

In the domain of self-improvement, achievement takes on a more thoughtful aspect. Health, education, and self-improvement goals become important benchmarks. For instance, actual wellness and prosperity are much of the time checked through measurements like weight, weight file (BMI), or execution in athletic pursuits. Degrees earned, certifications obtained, or the acquisition of new skills and knowledge are all indicators of educational success. It is becoming increasingly accepted that continuous learning and the pursuit of knowledge are important components of personal success. In a quickly impacting world, flexibility and a guarantee to remaining informed are fundamental characteristics that add to a singular's versatility and ability to explore difficulties.

In connections, achievement is much of the time estimated by the quality and profundity of associations with others. Significant connections, whether heartfelt, familial, or fellowships, contribute essentially to a singular's general prosperity. Effective communication, mutual support, trust, and shared values are indicators of successful relationships. The capacity to keep up with solid associations and explore relational difficulties mirrors an individual's capacity to understand people on a deeper level and social skill. Self-awareness, frequently seen as an inborn part of progress, includes mindfulness, versatility, and a readiness to stand up to and gain from mishaps. Beating hindrances and gaining from disappointments are necessary pieces of the excursion toward progress. A more robust and nuanced comprehension of achievement is facilitated by the capacity to adapt and persevere in the face of adversity.

While measurable metrics are useful for evaluating success, it's important to remember that success is a personal concept and that people's definitions can change over time. Social impacts, cultural assumptions, and individual qualities shape the standards against which achievement is estimated. As a result, people are encouraged to think about their own priorities, goals, and values in order to create a unique and meaningful understanding of success.

All in all, estimating achievement is a dynamic and emotional cycle that reaches out across different spaces of life. Success is frequently measured using a combination of tangible metrics and more intangible qualities like fulfillment, resilience, and personal development, whether in the professional, personal, or relational spheres. Perceiving the different variables that add to progress permits people to develop an all encompassing and customized comprehension of accomplishment that lines up with their qualities and desires.

# Key Performance Indicators (KPIs) for Holiday Marketing

Key Execution Pointers (KPIs) assume a critical part in evaluating the outcome of any showcasing methodology, and during the Christmas season, their importance turns out to be considerably more articulated. Successful occasion advertising requires cautious observing and investigation to guarantee that endeavors are lined up with business goals and reverberating with the interest group. How about we dive into the key KPIs that organizations ought to zero in on during their vacation promoting efforts.

**Change Rate:**

**Definition:** The level of site guests who complete an ideal activity, like making a buy, buying in, or finishing up a structure.

**Significance:** A high transformation rate demonstrates that the promoting messages are convincing and enticing, driving guests to make the ideal moves.

**Income Development:**

**Definition:** The overall increase in revenue compared to regular times during the holiday season.

**Significance:** A fundamental KPI, income development mirrors the viability of advertising endeavors in driving deals and expanding the by and large monetary strength of the business.

**Cost of acquiring a customer (CAC):**

**Definition:** the cost of acquiring a new client, including marketing costs.

**Significance:** Observing CAC guarantees that the expense of procuring new clients is legitimate according to the income created, adding to economic development.

**ROI (Return on Ad Spend):**

**Definition:** the proportion of advertising revenue to advertising expenditures.

**Significance:** ROSS gives bits of knowledge into the benefit of promoting efforts, permitting organizations to enhance their spending plan designation for greatest returns.

**Rates of email open and click-through:**

**Definition:** The proportion of recipients who open and use the links in marketing emails.

**Significance:** High open and navigate rates demonstrate that the email content is drawing in and important, adding to expanded site traffic and possible changes.

**Virtual Entertainment Commitment:**

**Definition:** The degree of connection (likes, remarks, shares) that virtual entertainment posts get.

**Significance:** Virtual entertainment commitment is a critical sign of brand mindfulness and crowd interest. Higher commitment recommends that the substance is resounding with the main interest group.

**Website Visitors:**

**Definition:** The quantity of guests to the site during the Christmas season.

**Significance:** The efficiency of marketing efforts in establishing an online presence and attracting attention from target audiences is demonstrated by an increase in website traffic.

**Client Consistency standard:**

**Definition:** The level of clients who keep on making buys after their underlying exchange.

**Significance:** Holding existing clients is essential for long haul achievement. A high consistency standard during special times of year demonstrates consumer loyalty and devotion.

**Normal Request Worth (AOV):**

**Definition:** The typical sum spent by clients in a solitary exchange.

**Significance:** Businesses can make strategic adjustments to increase revenue by understanding their customers' purchasing patterns through AOV monitoring.

**Stock Turnover:**

**Definition:** The times stock is sold and supplanted during a particular period.

**Significance:** For organizations managing actual items, enhancing stock turnover guarantees that items are available and promptly accessible to fulfill expanded occasion needs.

**Reviews and feedback from customers:**

**Definition:** the high-quality reviews and feedback from customers.

**Significance:** Checking client opinion gives important bits of knowledge into the general fulfillment with items and administrations, assisting organizations with making fundamental upgrades.

**Versatile Traffic and Changes:**

**Definition:** The level of site traffic and changes that happen on cell phones.

**Significance:** With the rising utilization of cell phones, following portable explicit KPIs guarantees that organizations take special care of the inclinations and ways of behaving of their versatile crowd.

Businesses looking to navigate and take advantage of holiday marketing opportunities need a thorough understanding of these key performance indicators. By carefully observing and dissecting these KPIs, organizations can go with information driven choices, streamline their procedures, and eventually make progress during the happy season.

# Analyzing and Adjusting Strategies

Breaking down and changing methodologies is an essential part of exploring the unique scenes of business, self-awareness, and different pursuits. The ability to evaluate and adjust your strategies is essential to success, whether you are leading a team, managing a project, or working toward personal objectives. We will investigate the significance of strategic analysis, the indicators that call for adjustments, and efficient strategies for fine-tuning them in this investigation.

At the center of any fruitful undertaking lies a very much created procedure. Nonetheless, a system is definitely not a static substance; It must adapt to new information and shifting circumstances. A comprehensive examination of the strategy's components, execution, and outcomes is required to evaluate its effectiveness. This procedure necessitates a thorough comprehension of the initial goals, the current setting, and the difficulties encountered along the way.

One basic part of vital investigation is assessing the arrangement between the system and the general objectives. This includes investigating whether the picked approach stays compatible with the mission and vision of the undertaking. A misalignment can prompt shortcomings, botched open doors, and a deviation from the ideal results. As a result, periodic evaluations are absolutely necessary to guarantee that the strategy continues to be an effective and relevant tool for achieving the desired outcomes.

Besides, breaking down key execution markers (KPIs) gives unmistakable measurements to check the progress of a technique. These markers could incorporate monetary measurements, consumer loyalty scores, or task achievements. By contrasting genuine execution against foreordained benchmarks, one can recognize solid areas and shortcoming inside the ongoing system. Metrics like website traffic, social media engagement, and conversion rates, for instance, become crucial when evaluating the effectiveness of a marketing strategy that aims to raise brand awareness.

The analysis relies heavily on qualitative feedback in addition to quantitative metrics. Stakeholders, team members, or customers can all provide valuable feedback on the strategy's perceived effectiveness. A comprehensive comprehension of the strategy's impact is made possible by this multifaceted evaluation, making it possible to make well-informed decisions about potential alterations.

The choice to change a technique frequently comes from perceiving disparities between the normal and real results. A new approach may be required due to external factors, market dynamics, or unanticipated obstacles. A company's marketing strategy or product positioning may need to be rethought, for instance, if it discovers that its product is not reaching the intended audience.

Also, amazing open doors might introduce themselves over the span of execution. These opportunities can be capitalized on by a flexible strategy that encourages growth and innovation. On the other hand, an unbending or obsolete methodology might impede an association from tackling the maximum capacity of an evolving scene.

Strategies must be altered in a way that strikes a delicate balance between change and continuity. While some aspects of the original strategy might work and should be kept, others might need to be changed or even completely changed. This cycle requests a readiness to embrace adaptability and a sharp familiarity with the developing setting in which the procedure works.

Viable correspondence is principal during the change stage. The reasons for the changes and the anticipated impact on the overall goals must be communicated to stakeholders, team members, and other relevant parties. All parties involved are aligned with the revised direction as a result of open communication, which fosters a sense of cohesion and comprehension.

Systems shouldn't just be changed responsively yet additionally proactively. It is possible to anticipate changes by regularly examining the external environment for trends, technological advancements, and competitive movements. This forward-looking methodology positions people and associations to remain on the ball, alleviating possible dangers and gaining by arising valuable open doors.

All in all, the iterative course of dissecting and changing procedures is a characteristic component of outcome in different spaces. A roadmap is provided by a well-executed strategy, but its effectiveness depends on its ability to adapt to changing circumstances. Through ceaseless assessment, arrangement with objectives, and responsiveness to input, people and associations can explore the intricacies of their interests with strength and dexterity.

# Chapter 9
# Case Studies and Successful Holiday

# Marketing Campaigns

Contextual investigations give important bits of knowledge into effective occasion showcasing efforts, offering a far reaching perspective on systems that resonated with shoppers and drove noteworthy outcomes. As organizations explore the serious scene of special seasons, looking at these examples of overcoming adversity can enlighten key standards and inventive methodologies that put crusades aside.

The Coca-Cola "Share a Coke" campaign is a notable example. This notorious occasion promoting drive customized the brand insight by supplanting its logo with famous names on Coca-Cola bottles. The campaign tapped into consumers' desire for individuality and created a sense of personal connection among them, making the product an appealing and shareable holiday gift. People eagerly shared images of their personalized Coke bottles, which resulted in a significant increase in sales and widespread social media engagement.

Likewise, Apple's vacation crusades reliably stand apart for their close to home reverberation and narrating. The tech monster capably joins item features with convincing stories that bring out a feeling of warmth and harmony. These campaigns go beyond the usual focus on the product to build a deeper, more personal connection between the brand and customers. Apple capitalizes on the holiday spirit to improve its brand image and increase sales by emphasizing themes of family, love, and shared experiences.

The progress of these missions highlights the significance of profound allure and personalization in occasion promoting. Customers are looking for more than just products; they look for encounters that resound with their qualities and feelings. Making stories that line up with the occasion soul while displaying items can make a strong mix that catches consideration and cultivates a positive brand affiliation.

Amazon's strategic use of data-driven insights during the holiday season is another compelling case study. Amazon's recommendation algorithms use its extensive database of customer preferences and actions to suggest personalized gifts. This designated approach works on the shopping experience for clients as well as improves the probability of effective exchanges. Amazon optimizes its marketing efforts by leveraging the power of data, ensuring that the appropriate products are presented to the appropriate audience at the appropriate time.

Starbucks' "12 Days of Christmas" campaign is an excellent illustration of using a countdown strategy to increase engagement and build anticipation. By presenting restricted time occasion themed items and advancements every day, Starbucks makes a feeling of energy and criticalness. This approach energizes everyday client connection and rehashed visits to find the most recent contributions. The restricted accessibility of these occasion things adds a component of selectiveness, driving interest and adding to the general outcome of the mission.

Powerhouse coordinated efforts have turned into a staple in present day promoting, and occasion crusades are no exemption. An essential case is the organization among Target and way of life powerhouses during the Christmas season. By organizing exceptional assortments as a team with famous powerhouses, Target grows its item range as well as takes advantage of the forces to be reckoned with committed fan base. This double pronged methodology consolidates the powerhouses' genuineness and reach with Target's image authority, bringing about expanded perceivability and deals during the happy period.

Additionally, the landscape of holiday marketing has been altered by the emergence of social media platforms. Brands like Nike influence client created content through occasion themed difficulties and missions. A sense of community and virality are both cultivated when customers are encouraged to share their holiday experiences with the brand. The force of client created content lies in its credibility, reverberating more firmly with expected clients than conventional publicizing.

These contextual investigations by and large feature the variety of effective occasion advertising methodologies, accentuating the significance of imagination, close to home reverberation, personalization, information driven experiences, and vital joint efforts. Studying these success stories provides a roadmap for crafting compelling narratives, authentically engaging with customers, and ultimately achieving a memorable and impactful holiday presence for businesses planning their campaigns.

# Lessons Learned and Best Practices

In the domain of occasion promoting, utilizing the bubbly soul of Christmas can be a strong impetus for business development. As the years progressed, organizations have learned important examples and recognized prescribed procedures to explore the Christmas season effectively. Here, we dive into key methodologies for occasion promoting achievement, investigating the subtleties of taking advantage of holiday spirit for ideal business results.

**Figuring out the Force of Feeling**

Vital to occasion advertising achievement is perceiving the profound reverberation of Christmas. It's a period related with happiness, warmth, and fellowship. Organizations that inject their advertising systems with these feelings are bound to reverberate with their crowd.

Brands can use storytelling as a powerful tool to connect with customers on a personal level. Sharing stories that inspire sentimentality or convey the soul of giving can manufacture a more profound close to home bond.

**Making Content That Is Both Engaging and Festive Content** is still king in the digital age, and during the holidays, it takes on a more festive tone. Businesses need to make an investment in creating content that enthralls and entertains customers, whether it's heartwarming videos, visually appealing graphics, or interactive social media campaigns. Coordinating Christmas subjects into advertising materials catches consideration as well as adjusts the brand to the happy feelings of the time.

## Personalization for a Customized Insight

One-size-fits-all showcasing approaches miss the mark during special times of year. Personalization is vital to hanging out in the packed merry scene. Understanding client inclinations and conduct permits organizations to tailor their advertising endeavors.

The objective is to cultivate customer loyalty that lasts beyond the holiday season through personalized email campaigns and targeted promotions that make customers feel valued and appreciated.

## Consistent Omni-Channel Insight

In the present interconnected world, clients anticipate a consistent encounter across different channels. Occasion showcasing achievement relies on making a durable brand presence that ranges physical and computerized touchpoints. Coordinating on the web and disconnected systems guarantees that clients can easily change from finding a bubbly proposal via virtual entertainment to making a buy coming up or on the web.

## Timing Is Everything

The Christmas season is set apart by a whirlwind of exercises, and organizations should be vital in their timing. Sending off crusades too soon may bring about weakness, while a postponed start could mean passing up urgent open doors. Figuring out the perfect balance requires grasping the way of behavior of the interest group and adjusting promoting endeavors to key achievements, like the huge shopping day after Thanksgiving or The online Christmas sales extravaganza.

## Saddling the Force of Virtual Entertainment

Online entertainment stages act as virtual town squares during special times of year. Businesses are more likely to succeed if they take advantage of the reach and engagement potential of social media platforms like Instagram, Facebook, and Twitter. The brand's visibility and impact are increased by creating shareable content, hosting festive contests, and actively engaging with customers through comments and messages.

## Underscoring Worth and Offering in return

While advancements and limits are fundamental to occasion showcasing, stressing the worth of items or administrations goes past financial contemplations. The promotional message gains weight when the quality, uniqueness, or exclusivity of the offerings are emphasized. Additionally, aligning the brand with the spirit of giving that characterizes Christmas is accomplished by incorporating a charitable element, such as donating a portion of sales to a relevant cause.

The ongoing process of iteratively analyzing data serves as the foundation for holiday marketing strategies. Organizations ought to intently screen crusade execution, client conduct, and market patterns. By utilizing examination devices, advertisers can distinguish what works and what doesn't, empowering them to make information driven changes progressively. Every holiday season builds on previous successes and insights through iterative learning.

**Offsetting Merriment with Brand Consistency**

While embracing the occasional soul, keeping up with brand consistency is critical. The happy components ought to supplement the brand's personality as opposed to eclipse it. Finding some kind of harmony guarantees that clients perceive and resound with the brand, even amidst occasional festivals.

An essential component of holiday marketing success is anticipating and preparing for increased demand. Whether it's guaranteeing adequate stock, enhancing site execution for higher traffic, or increasing client care, organizations should be prepared to fulfill the flood in need that frequently goes with the Christmas season.

Successful holiday marketing strategies require a delicate balance between personalization, strategic execution, and emotion. Businesses can create campaigns that not only boost short-term sales but also cultivate long-term customer relationships by comprehending the distinctive dynamics of the Christmas season.

As innovation develops and shopper ways of behaving shift, the illustrations learned and best practices recognized in occasion showcasing will keep on molding the scene of bubbly business into the indefinite future.

# CONCLUSION

## Looking Ahead to Future Holiday Seasons

The landscape of holiday marketing is constantly changing, which presents businesses seeking to capitalize on the holiday spirit for growth with both challenges and opportunities. As we look forward to future special seasons, perceiving the powerful idea of purchaser conduct and the rising meaning of computerized stages in molding buying decisions is pivotal.

One of the vital techniques for occasion promoting achievement is embracing a multi-channel approach. Businesses must adapt and engage across a variety of platforms, including social media, e-commerce websites, and mobile apps, as consumers diversify their online interactions. Making durable and convincing stories that reverberate with the crowd across these channels can make a consistent and vivid experience, encouraging more grounded associations between the brand and buyers.

Besides, personalization arises as a crucial calculation occasion. Customer engagement and loyalty are enhanced when campaigns are tailored to individual preferences and actions. Businesses can gain valuable insights into consumer preferences by utilizing data analytics and artificial intelligence, allowing them to provide personalized content, recommendations, and promotions. This makes a more pleasant shopping experience as well as improves the probability of transformation.

The ascent of supportability cognizance adds one more layer to occasion advertising systems. Brands that are socially and environmentally responsible are increasingly appealing to consumers. Incorporating reasonable practices into occasion crusades lines up with moral commercialization as well as mirrors a pledge to corporate social obligation. Businesses can use sustainability as a unique selling point to appeal to a growing segment of conscious consumers by offering eco-friendly packaging and charitable efforts.

It is impossible to overstate the significance of storytelling in today's digital age. Making stories that inspire feeling and interface with the crowd on an individual level can separate a brand during the Christmas season. Businesses can use storytelling to create memorable experiences that leave a lasting impression on customers through heartwarming videos, nostalgic content, or user-generated stories.

In addition, the power of influencer marketing as a tool for holiday promotion is only getting stronger. Teaming up with powerhouses who line up with the brand's qualities and resound with the main interest group can intensify reach and validity. Utilizing forces to be reckoned with to exhibit occasion items or offer individual encounters makes credible associations and assembles trust among purchasers.

Utilizing the potential of augmented reality (AR) and virtual reality (VR) technologies can provide innovative and immersive experiences as we prepare for upcoming holiday seasons. AR-driven take a stab at highlights, virtual occasion enhancements, or intuitive missions can enthrall crowds and separate a brand in a packed commercial center. Keeping up to date with mechanical progressions and integrating them into occasion techniques positions organizations at the bleeding edge of development.

Holiday marketing faces both challenges and opportunities as a result of globalization of commerce. Fitting efforts to resound with different social practices and customs is fundamental for brands growing their span to global business sectors. Language confinement, social responsiveness, and understanding territorial inclinations add to the outcome of occasion crusades on a worldwide scale.

adaptability, creativity, and a thorough comprehension of changing consumer habits are essential for holiday marketing's future success. Embracing a multi-channel, customized approach, incorporating supportability practices, and excelling at narrating are basic parts of an effective occasion promoting technique. Businesses that explore new frontiers like augmented and virtual reality will remain ahead of the curve as technology continues to advance.

The future of festive marketing will be shaped by the combination of cutting-edge technology and traditional holiday charm. Organizations that explore this offset with imagination and understanding won't just celebrate occasional achievement yet in addition develop enduring associations with purchasers in the consistently advancing commercial center.